CW01024098

THE
SCOTTISH INTERIOR

DAVID RAMSAY HAY 1798–1866 WITH HIS DOG, BRUSH
— *Scotland's first Interior Decorator* —

THE
SCOTTISH INTERIOR

GEORGIAN AND VICTORIAN DECOR

*A Visual Anthology of the Domestic Room
in Scotland culled principally from the Collections of the
National Monuments Record of Scotland*

IAN GOW

With a Preface by John Cornforth

EDINBURGH UNIVERSITY
PRESS

*For
Margaret
Swain*

© Ian Gow, 1992
Published by Edinburgh University Press
22 George Square, Edinburgh

Designed by Dalrymple
Typeset in Adobe New Caledonia by Koinonia, Bury
Reproduction by Technic Color Separation Ltd, Hong Kong
Printed and Bound by
The Bath Press Ltd

British Library Cataloguing in Publication Data
Gow, Ian
The Scottish Interior: Georgian and Victorian decor.
I. Title
747.22
ISBN 0 7486 0220 8 (cased)

*The publisher gratefully acknowledges subsidy from the Scottish Arts Council
towards the publication of this volume.*

FOREWORD

The collections of the National Monuments Record of Scotland form one of the most comprehensive sources of information on archaeological and architectural topics in Scotland. Since 1966 when the National Buildings Record of Scotland and the Royal Commission on the Ancient and Historical Monuments were amalgamated, the range and scale of the collections have greatly increased. There are two aspects to the Commission's work: firstly there is the ongoing programme of fieldwork, covering structures of every type from prehistoric farmsteads to de-commissioned nuclear power-stations and football stadia; secondly, there is the duty laid on the founders of the Record in 1941 to preserve earlier historical material of every kind, including early survey and architectural survey drawings as well as manuscripts relating to Scotland's historic architecture. Coverage has been augmented by copying material in private collections, thus making it more readily available to students, and at the same time a number of important Scottish collections have been attracted, like those of

the Royal Incorporation of Architects in Scotland. This vast body of material forms the core of data and illustration drawn on by Ian Gow for this book.

In recent years the Commision has sought to make this storehouse of information available to as wide a public as possible through its own publications, through exhibitions and by encouraging personal research in the Record. We are thus delighted to take part in helping to make this hitherto unexplored aspect of the collections more widely known, and similar collaborations between the Press and the Commission are set to continue in other fields. The volume capitalises on the longstanding personal interest of Ian Gow, the Curator of Architecture, whose energies have done so much to increase the range of the collections. The illustrations published here, many for the first time, testify to the current strengths of the Record. I hope very much that this volume will lead to further accessions to and research within the collections, the enhancement and curation of which is the central duty of the Commission.

Roger J. Mercer
Secretary to the Royal Commission on the Ancient and Historical Monuments of Scotland
Curator of the National Monuments Record of Scotland

RCAHMS

An Englishman may not be able to struggle through the novels of Sir Walter Scott, but he will have no such difficulty with Ian Gow's *The Scottish Interior*. Indeed he will feel like a Sassenach Oliver Twist asking for more. It is not that this helping is not substantial enough, but it is clear that the author has a great deal more to say about the Scottish interior from the late seventeenth century and could put what he sees as the high point of interest in the early nineteenth century into a broader as well as a more detailed context. There are many tempting references to D. R. Hay (1798–1866), who, thanks to Ian Gow's researches, is shown to be Scotland's first interior decorator and a figure with as yet no English equivalent. Suitably he had a hand in Abbotsford, the key Scottish house.

From Ian Gow's point of view a book of this kind is a cross between a lucky dip and a paper chase, because while he has probably found a great deal more views than he expected, particularly early photographs going back to the late 1850s (many of them in the admirable National Monuments Record for Scotland), he has found fewer amateur drawings than he hoped. This suggests that drawing masters may not have had such extensive practices in Scotland as in England, because there would certainly have been more days when late Regency and early Victorian ladies must have gazed disconsolately out of drawing room windows at the grey drizzle and wished they had something else to do other than sew and read their novels. On the other hand, he has taken a broader social view than Mario Praz did in his *History of Decoration* and than I attempted in *Quest for Comfort*, because he is concerned with the interior, and not just with decoration, and so interiors of great houses are combined with those of humble cottages and Edinburgh slums.

Although it is not possible to demonstrate in this book, because there are so few illustrations like the drawing for the Great Drawing Room at Blair Castle of 1758, the eighteenth-century Scottish interior has a distinctive character. That is particularly apparent in the handling of woodwork and plasterwork, and, largely thanks to the pioneering work of the much-missed Francis Bamford, through some of its furniture as well. However what no one has yet done is to pursue the collecting of pictures in Scotland and consider how broadly based that was in the eighteenth and nineteenth centuries. There are still a surprising number of distinguished collections in Scotland, and it would be interesting to know more about the relationship between pictures and furniture in late eighteenth- and early nineteenth-century Edinburgh and Glasgow houses. In England our view is dominated by country houses and, even now, remarkably little is known about London interiors, particularly those in the houses of professional men. Fashion in England was set by London, but in Edinburgh in the late eighteenth and nineteenth centuries the top was different: lacking a court and a parliament, it was dominated by people with a professional background, who created their own world and in the process encouraged local firms specialising in furnishing and decoration, like Trotter of Edinburgh. It may be that Scotsmen set more store by pictures and spent more on them than we realise. Certainly the illustrations in this book appear to bear this out, and it would be fascinating to know more about the quality of what is seen hanging on the walls in houses like that of David Anderson of Moredun, whose Edinburgh rooms were photographed in 1858. A simpler but revealing example from the mid 1890s is William Reid's apartment above his business, Morison and Co. of George Street, cabinet makers and upholsterers: he evidently collected both Old Master etchings and eighteenth-century mezzotints.

The character of the Scottish interior was quite complicated, because while the professional classes and the gentry were almost entirely Scottish in their orientation, there was also a smaller circle of greater landowners who looked to London architects and employed London firms, like Dowbiggin, who furnished William Burn's new rooms at Saltoun Hall in 1822. They would have sent their goods north by sea before the coming of the railways.

The lack of a court and the sense of being deprived of its rightful history was in fact an important element in the Scottish attitude. One of the most fascinating aspects of this book is the way that attitudes to the Palace of Holyroodhouse are demonstrated from the time of George IV down to Queen Mary, incidentally explaining how the irritating back-to-front aspect of the state rooms in the palace came about. It is also revealing to see how mid nineteenth-century Holyrood is tied up with the Queen's love of Balmoral, which is recorded in some of the best watercolours in the book, by James Giles. Indeed it is pity that he and Robert Gibb do not seem to have painted more interiors.

Although a Scot, Ian Gow always takes a questioning view of accepted Scottish attitudes to the Scottish tradition and he is particularly good on how and why they developed. So it is logical that he includes a few plates from historic books on Scottish architecture such as Billing's *Baronial and Ecclesiastical Antiquities of Scotland* (1845–52), because they have had such a great influence on the Scottish view of its own architecture, not least on Lorimer's interpretation of it. It is good to be able to compare those plates with early photographs, as with Winton, but since Ian Gow is rightly against what he calls the 'rubble look', I miss a photograph of the Great Hall at Glamis that would explain how much of its dramatic character is owed to the Italianate taste of the Countess of Strathmore, the wife of the 14th Earl and the mother of Queen Elizabeth the Queen Mother.

Many of the illustrations are of places that have gone, and, while it is right that Ian Gow should have kept away from photographs taken by *Country Life* as much as possible, it is fascinating to see earlier records of Hamilton Palace in 1882, before the great sale. And there are other unexpected bonuses, like a photograph of the Great Drawing Room at Drumlanrig Castle when it was hung with tapestry. It is only to be regretted that Bedford Lemere did not make more sorties north of the border, because his set of Charles Rennie Mackintosh's Hill House, Helensburgh, taken in 1904, is outstanding. Sometimes a picture or piece of furniture hops out because one can recognise it from another house, as with Montgomerie in Ayrshire from which the contents migrated to Longnor in Shropshire and were photographed there by *Country Life* 1963. Those are some of the details that show that while this particular chase of Ian Gow's is over, the process will continue; hopefully the book will lead to the emergence of more views from all sorts of strange places.

fig 1
Sir Walter Scott
in Mary Queen of Scots'
bedroom at Holyrood

The academic study of historic interiors owes much to the publications of the old Furniture and Woodwork Department at the Victoria and Albert Museum when it was under the inspiring leadership of Peter Thornton. During a spell with the Inspectorate of Ancient Monuments in London, I had the privilege of benefiting not only from his advice but that of his colleagues John Hardy, Simon Jervis, Maurice Tomlin and Clive Wainwright. The books and copious *Country Life* articles of John Cornforth have been of equal importance and I have been fortunate to benefit from conversations with him on his Scottish excursions. I am most grateful to him for supplying the Preface to this book.

In Scotland my initial search for views of Scottish rooms was inspired by Desmond Hodges who asked me to lecture on the original appearance of the houses of Edinburgh's New Town. This book also owes much to Sheila MacKay and Nic Allen of the Moubray House Press who published the first selection of views in their pioneering *Scottish Interiors* Series. I am also grateful to the staffs of the following institutions for their help in chasing illustrations or arranging for copies to be made. They include the British Architectural Library, Edinburgh Public Libraries, the National Art Library, the National Library of Scotland, the Scottish Record Office and the Royal Library.

My search for views of Scottish Rooms has been made both easier and more enjoyable through the kind assistance of many friends and colleagues. Duncan Bull, Mungo Campbell, Timothy Clifford, Dr Lindsay Errington, James Holloway, Margaret Kelly, Susanna Kerr, Julie Lawson, Hugh Macandrew, Fiona Pearson, Antonia Reeve, Helen Smailes and Sara Stevenson have all guided me through the collections of the National Galleries of Scotland. Dr Iain Gordon Brown has been equally helpful at the National Library of Scotland while Hugh Cheape, Virginia Glenn and Naomi Tarrant have rendered assistance at the National Museums of Scotland. At the National Trust for Scotland, John Batty, Christopher Hartley, David Learmont and Caroline Neave have directed me to many things I should otherwise have missed and smoothed the way for our photographers. At Historic Buildings and Monuments, I am particularly grateful to Rebecca Barker, Richard Emerson, Richard Fawcett, Anne Riches, Rab Snowden, and Dr David Walker.

The majority of the illustrations in this book come from the collections of the National Monuments Record of Scotland where it is my privilege to work and this book would not have been possible without the ready access to this material. In developing the collections in recent years I have been building on the sure foundations established during the early 1950s by the late Colin McWilliam, who is sadly missed, and Kitty Cruft, the recently retired Curator. I am very pleased that the Royal Commission on the Ancient and Historical Monuments of Scotland have agreed to sponsor this publication and I would like to record my gratitude to the Chairman, Lord Crawford and the Commissioners. The book owes much to the interest of the Secretary, Roger Mercer and his predecessor, J G Dunbar, as well as to the kindness of the two Commissioners who share especial responsibility for the Record, Mrs P E Durham and the Hon. Lord Cullen. Although it is invidious to identify individuals on the Commission staff because everything that we do is the result of a team effort I would like to thank especially Janet Christie, Simon Green, Gillian Haggart, Gordon Maxwell, Shona McGaw, Christine McWilliam, Geoffrey Quick, Harriet Richardson, Charlie Scott, Jane Thomas, Louise Torrance and Ruth Wimberley, while Ann Martin and Robert Adam deserve especial praise for providing copy prints for publication from often indifferent originals.

For general advice and practical help with specific illustrations I am indebted to Sheena Andrew, Zelda Ashford, Maurice Berrill, David Black, Laurance Black, Dr Stephanie Blackden, Dorothy Bosomworth, Margaret Campbell, Jim Clark, Dr Tristram Clarke, Rob Close, the late Mrs Margie Cross, Dr Elizabeth Cumming, Althea Dundas-Bekker, Professor David and Francina Irwin, John Gerrard, Christopher Gilbert, Ierne Grant, Elspeth Hardie, Dr Malcolm Higgs and Margaret Gilfillan of the Architectural Heritage Society of Scotland, Jack Howells, Martin Hopkinson, Colin Johnston, David Jones, Wendy Kaplan, Shelagh Kennedy, Juliet Kinchin, Ewan Lamont, Hew Lorimer, Dr

James Macaulay, Dr Sam McKinstry, Charles McKean and the staff of the Royal Incorporation of Architects in Scotland, Dr Duncan Macmillan, The Earl of Mansfield, Sarah Medlam, The Earl of Moray, William Payne, the late John Pinkerton, Geraldine Prince, Sebastian Pryke, Campbell Reid, Harriet Richardson, The Hon Jane Roberts, Joe Rock, Hugh Ross, Professor Alistair Rowan, Sally Rush, David Scarratt, James Simpson, Gavin Stamp, Henrietta Stephen, Elizabeth Strong who lent many books, Ailsa Tanner, Peter Thornton, Ben Tindall, Dr David, Averil and David Walker, and Donald Wickes. Oliver Barratt kindly lent me a typewriter at a critical moment, Margaret Swain, with her unshakeable belief in the intrinsic merit of the decorative arts of Scotland has been such a tower of strength that I have dedicated the book to her.

The preparation of the book owes much to the enthusiasm of Vivian Bone, Helen Simms and the late Martin Spencer at Edinburgh University Press and to its designer, Robert Dalrymple. Lastly, I am grateful to my family for tolerating the reduction of one particular Scottish interior to chaos under tottering piles of photographs and reference books for longer than I should have wished.

Ian Gow

The National Monuments Record of Scotland

fig 2
Carved stone fragment bearing a late medieval domestic scene found in Cockburn Street, Edinburgh. Drawn by Thomas Ross 1879

INTRODUCTION

The Scottish Interior may not seem a very promising subject. The tenacious conventional view remains that the Scots foreswore everything that smacked of luxury in their houses under the astringent influence of John Knox and that their only contribution to interior design had to await the genius of Charles Rennie Mackintosh. Even this late flowering has been subject to the national talent for self-denigration because Mackintosh was depicted as a martyr to Scottish philistinism. In fact nothing could be further from the truth and, if trouble is taken to look , there is plenty of evidence to show that the Scots were no less interested in the comfort and beauty of their houses than any other nation in Europe.

The myth has been powerful enough to discourage research but in his pioneering *Domestic Life in Scotland 1488-1688*, published in 1920, John Warrack examined one important source of documentary evidence. By relating inventories of domestic chattels, usually taken on the death of their owner, to surviving examples of furniture and embroidery, Warrack built up a composite picture of the Scottish house which proved that it was far from unsophisticated. This book also concentrates on a single source and endeavours to bring together the surviving contemporary visual records of Scottish rooms. It therefore follows in the footsteps of Mario Praz and such subsequent southern scholarship as John Cornforth's

English Interiors 1790–1848 (1978) and Peter Thornton's *Authentic Decor* (1984). Although it includes drawings as well as photographs, it is most closely modelled on William Seale's study of photographs of American interiors, *The Tasteful Interlude* (1975) because I have tried to bring together a similar range of examples from Palaces to cottages and even slums, with occasional visits to hotels.

We can , of course, only go where the draughtsman or photographer has been. At the outset it is worth reminding ourselves of the limitations of this method. These views, although arranged in chronological order, can never add up to a history of Scottish interior decoration. They do, however, constitute a history of the recording of the Scottish interior, and this has emerged as an important sub theme. The simple concept for us of making a record of a room in the form of a perspective sketch seems to have taken a surprisingly long time to develop. During the eighteenth century architects presented their designs in the more architectural form of the section (see page 15, for example), which has the merit of enabling the dimensions to be read off easily. An important exception, however, is the decorative perspective engraving of the Chapel Royal at Holyrood which William Adam included in *Vitruvius Scoticus*. Taken from a view by the artist Jan Wyck (1652–1700)

fig 3
'Inside of the Chappell Royal of Holyroodhouse' from *Vitruvius Scoticus*

its perspective presentation, like a further plate of the exterior of Kinross House, is unusual in comparison to Adam's presentation of his own designs.

In this book I have eschewed both portraits which incidentally introduce domestic detail and conversation pieces. Although they both constitute a vital source for earlier periods, in the absence of any comparative visual information, there is now a growing tendency among historians of the decorative arts to treat them with caution. In the portraits the details are often drawn from stock to reflect accomplishments on the sitters, while in the conversation pieces each element in the picture has been accrued to further the storyline. Even so popular painting as Alexander Carse's *Arrival of the Country Relations* of 1812, is not, in my view, as 'realistic' as it may seem. In his anxiety to show the urban context, Carse underlines the point with two windows whose placing would be unusual in reality and he dispenses with curtains for the sake of clarity.

A few furniture plans have been included in the book to show how its disposition influenced the way in which rooms were depicted. It is significant that the eighteenth-century formal arrangement broke down at the same time as the perspective came into common usage. Both of these features may be a product of the dominance of the Picturesque aesthetic.

In England, once the tradition of artists making perspective records of interiors had been established, a large number of amateurs began to make watercolours of their homes. Curiously the Scots do not seem to have pursued this hobby with equal enthusiasm and there is not the same wealth of examples to draw on. It may simply be that Scotland abounded in more stimulating Picturesque subject matter.

Even after the invention of photography the field stays surprisingly limited. Once the obvious difficulties of recording interiors had been overcome, a variety of factors, including propriety, restricted the subjects deemed suitable for the Victorian photographer. We must also remain alert to the photographer's active participation in orchestrating the arrangement of the furniture as an unusual pair of photographs of Duff House reveals (see figs 5 and 6). Even when the snapshot became a reality through technical advances, remarkably few people bothered to direct their cameras to the interiors of their own homes. Photograph albums all too often follow the pattern of earlier Scottish sketchbooks and I would willingly swop a hundred views of Melrose Abbey for a single photograph of a scullery.

Inevitably, the majority of the illustrations show the houses of the rich and famous. During the search I have longed to find a record of an 'ordinary' house but this is a

fig 4
'The Arrival of the Country Relations'
Alexander Carse

fruitless quest because the very act of making a drawing or taking a photograph proved that there was something extraordinary about it. The paradox emerged, however, that in their pursuit of the exotic, Victorian photographers often unwittingly recorded the ordinary, as in the case of King Duncan's alleged Bedroom at Cawdor Castle (see page 142). Perhaps even more extraordinary, the four views that for us are now a rare record of a very average country house turn out to have been made because of Ballechin's notoriety as the 'Most Haunted House' in Scotland (see figs 7 and 8).

In spite of these limitations the aim of this book remains a worthwhile exercise. With all faults, the illustrations reproduced here do show the interiors as their occupants wished them to be seen. Modern photographs of historic rooms can never possess the same immediacy because they betray later changes. It is fundamentally improbable that a single item of furniture has occupied the same spot in Scotland since the sixteenth century and the saga of Mary Queen of Scots' Bedroom at Holyrood serves as a warning to those who believe otherwise (see pages 44–47).

I have also chosen to reject designs for interiors because it soon became clear that this should be the subject of another book. Designs now seem every bit as rare as record drawings but this is because no Scottish National Institution ever sought to preserve them until recently and so Scotland has nothing to match the resources of the Royal Institute of British Architects or the Victoria and Albert Museum who have been collecting actively since the mid-nineteenth century.

Frustratingly, I have failed to locate a number of interior views which I know exist. The saddest gap must be the lithographs of Hendersyde Park at Kelso. These are mentioned in the almost insanely detailed catalogues to its collections which were published in 1835 and 1859 and written by its owner, John Waldie, who appears to list the contents of every drawer. Although John Harris noted the passage of a set through the international art market they have gone to ground and, because the house has been demolished, we must await their reappearance to discover what this grouping of modern Neo-Classical sculpture, a picture collection strong on hopeful attributions and massive furniture by Mein, the local cabinet maker, was like.

Although I have provided notes to the illustrations, I hope that this anthology will speak for itself and appeal to a wide variety of people who bring different interests to the Scottish Interior. I also hope that it might encourage a few of its readers to undertake the more detailed research which is badly needed and which I believe should prove rewarding.

In 1986, I organised a conference on the Scottish Interior for the Architectural Heritage Society of Scotland and the extra-mural Department of Edinburgh University and was surprised at the enthusiasm which it generated both within Scotland and in the South. Because the conference was primarily addressed to the protection of historic interiors there was insufficient time to deal with the vernacular interior but in 1989 a conference on this theme was organised by the Scottish Vernacular Buildings Working Group and it was clear

figs 5 & 6, above
This unusual pair of photographs of Duff House *c.*1870 reveal the extent to which the photographer could rearrange a room to suit his own ideas of composition.

figs 7 & 8, opposite
Photographic survey of Ballechin House from an extra-illustrated copy of *The Alleged Haunting of B—— House*, 1900.

that this area is the subject of such intensive scholarship that it has emerged as a specialist area.

Because this book deals with a broad range of interiors, I am conscious that I can only touch on vernacular interiors and attempt to show the range of sources that exist in Scotland. I am also aware that the boom in photography during the 1890s, which I have tried to reflect here, through amateurs swelling the ranks and the commercial viability of photographic reproductions in books and magazines, makes it difficult to choose examples. This also makes it almost impossible to attempt coverage of the twentieth century, and it is equally difficult to take a balanced view of relatively modern times. Sadly a very great deal of more recent material had to be left out for reasons of space and my publisher's peace of mind but they have nobly entertained the idea of an expanded edition if there is sufficient interest.

Front Hall.

THE ALLEGED HAUNTING

OF B—— HOUSE

Upper Gallery.

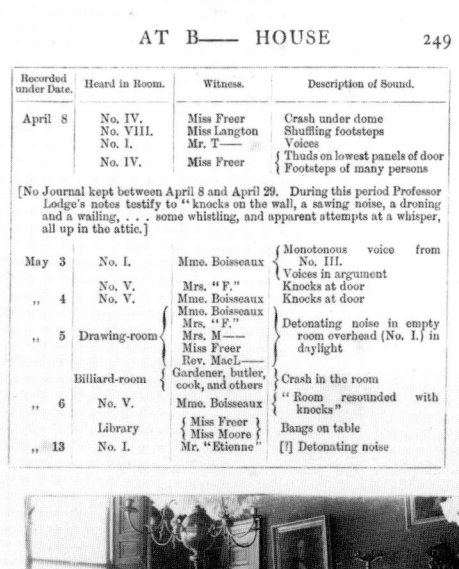

AT B—— HOUSE   249

Recorded under Date.	Heard in Room.	Witness.	Description of Sound.
April 8	No. IV.	Miss Freer	Crash under dome
	No. VIII.	Miss Langton	Shuffling footsteps
	No. I.	Mr. T——	Voices
	No. IV.	Miss Freer	Thuds on lowest panels of door / Footsteps of many persons

[No Journal kept between April 8 and April 29. During this period Professor Lodge's notes testify to "knocks on the wall, a sawing noise, a droning and a wailing, . . . some whistling, and apparent attempts at a whisper, all up in the attic.]

May 3	No. I.	Mme. Boisseaux	Monotonous voice from No. III. / Voices in argument
	No. V.	Mrs. "F."	Knocks at door
„ 4	No. V.	Mme. Boisseaux	Knocks at door
„ 5	Drawing-room	Mme. Boisseaux / Mrs. "F." / Mrs. M—— / Miss Freer / Rev. MacI.—	Detonating noise in empty room overhead (No. I.) in daylight
	Billiard-room	Gardener, butler, cook, and others	Crash in the room
„ 6	No. V.	Mme. Boisseaux	"Room resounded with knocks"
	Library	Miss Freer / Miss Moore	Bangs on table
„ 13	No. I.	Mr. "Etienne"	[?] Detonating noise

Dining room.

1: THE LIBRARY AT ARNISTON HOUSE BY WILLIAM ADAM
1726

The nine plates of interiors in William Adam's *Vitruvius Scoticus* are the first published views of Scottish rooms and testify to his deep interest in the decoration of his houses. The Library is presented in diagrammatic form as an exploded section with elevations of the four walls grouped around the plan. This form of presentation was probably copied from the engraved plates of interiors published in Colen Campbell's *Vitruvius Britannicus*. It was also the method adopted by Adam in presenting designs for interiors to his patrons, although the library here is labelled as if it was a topographical view rather than a design. The curious proportions and spacing of the windows arise from its situation at the top of the house, behind the pediment of the principal front. The skied library was to become a popular feature of eighteenth-century Scottish country houses and the grandeur of Adam's design for Arniston must have helped to establish this fashion. The treatment is characteristic of Adam in its architectural rigour with its Ionic pilasters under a correctly pulvinated frieze. He achieved extra height by breaking the cove up into the roofspace which is typical of his almost organic approach

to planning buildings. His fondness for sculptural enrichment here takes the form of a set of carefully placed library busts within arcading which ingeniously bridges the differential spacing of the windows. In execution the pendentives were given stucco enrichments and birds enliven the chimneypiece whose simpler form, with marble slips framing a looking glass in its upper tier, was a favourite design which was stocked by his marble works in Leith. The glazed cases must have been a luxurious novelty in the 1720s and the design demonstrates those inventive powers which made Adam Scotland's most successful architect. Although the hatching captures the bold modelling of the interior, a black and white engraving cannot recapture the liveliness of Adam's rooms whose effect depended on their decorative painting. The real and often exotic marbles of his chimneypieces were accompanied by imitation painted marble and graining. Today the Library at Arniston is oak grained but accounts show it was originally finished in white and gold. In spite of Adam's careful preparation, his book was not published until *c.*1811 although the plates must have circulated earlier.

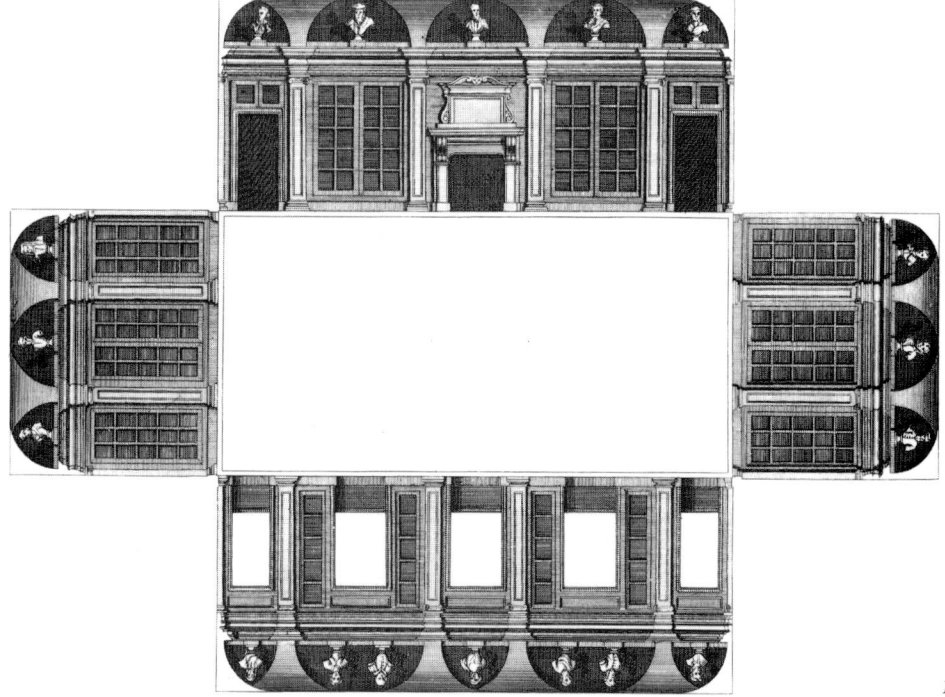

1b

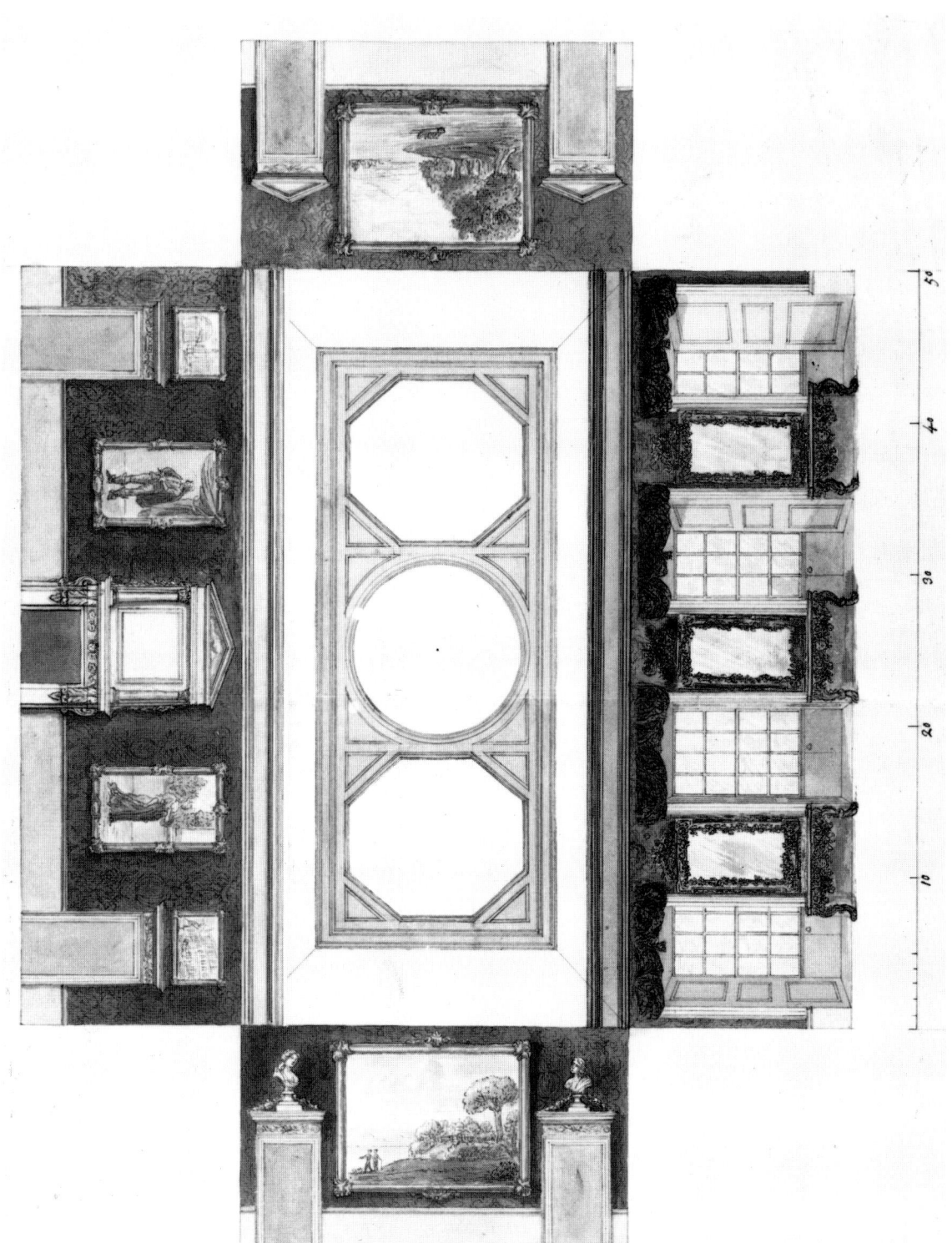

2: DESIGN FOR FITTING UP THE GREAT DRAWING ROOM
AT BLAIR CASTLE BY STEUARD MACKENZIE ESQ.
1758

At first glance this design appears to conform to the standard eighteenth-century way of visualising a room as a set of exploded elevations but it has unusual features which suggest that it cannot be the work of a professional architect whilst still adding greatly to its value as a source of information about decorative practice. Comparison with Adam's view of Arniston shows that here the artist has eccentrically grouped the elevations around the ceiling rather than the floor plan while the window wall is shown in perspective. The use of realistic colour is usually thought to have been an innovation of Robert Adam. Whoever the designer was, the architect had already ensured that the Great Drawing Room, in spite of being formed within old walls, should have a dignity appropriate to an important state room by providing symmetrically placed doors and a central chimneypiece, A fashionable Palladian cove has been provided and the only feature which betrays that this is not a modern room is the even number of windows where three or five would be more correct. Because its configuration is so like the present drawing room this must be a design for fitting it up as the three alternative doorcases suggest. Pictures were essential to create a magnificent effect and the room has been designed to show them off in a formal arrangement with gilded *en suite* frames with Baroque ornaments. The big Italianate scenes for the end walls would have had to be commissioned especially for the room. The two full-length portraits, interestingly, are hung to face the big landscapes rather than each other as we would automatically do today. The walls are hung with silk damask which was essential for such a grand drawing room but which also provided an excellent foil to the pictures. The artist has indicated that the red damask was to have a very long repeat like that which still survives in the Red Drawing Room at Hopetoun. The draw-up curtains are shown in matching silk and are pulled tightly against their pulleyboards. The only furnishings depicted are the triad of three gilded looking-glasses with pier tables below the white marble tops of which match the chimneypiece. These important pieces were often designed by architects and thus appear on such drawings whereas the seat furniture which was upholstered in the same silk as the walls took a secondary place in such a scheme. Because of this, and the fact that they were conventionally ranged against the walls in a formal pattern, seat furniture was often omitted from architectural designs during this period. The yellow on the ceiling panels is probably intended to indicate that its ornaments were to be gilded like the frames and pier tables; this was a prerequisite for important drawing rooms in order to show their state-room status. All these idiosyncrasies make this drawing a particularly vivid impression of the grandeur expected in such an important room.

Facing: 2

3: THE FOULIS ACADEMY IN THE COLLEGE, GLASGOW
c.1760

Although not strictly domestic, it would be unthinkable not to include this remarkable, but problematic, engraving of the Foulis Academy in a book devoted to the Scottish Interior. The view is usually attributed to David Allan, who was the School's most brilliant pupil, and there is a related oil painting in the Hunterian Museum. The Foulis Academy was an innovative educational experiment for the training of young apprentice artists. It was established by the Foulis brothers who are best known for their elegant printed books, but who also founded the art collection displayed here for the use of their young students. Their Academy enjoyed the support of prominent Glasgow merchants who looked to it for a source of designs for their manufacturing enterprises. This worthy venture was granted accommodation in the ground storey of William Adam's new Library at the College. Although the disposition of the space relates to Adam's published design, the scale has been greatly exaggerated, but this would perhaps be understandable as a devoted student's-eye view of this unusual institution and it is interesting that this rare, early attempt at an interior view should have been generated in the Foulis Academy. It is perhaps unwise to place any very great reliance on the details but the pineapple chandeliers, the curtains with their lambrequin valance, the bookcases with their dust flaps and the rococo glass on the pier being used to reflect light towards the engraver, may all have had parallels in contemporary Glasgow interiors although the chair looks a trifle improbable. Part of the awkwardness of the scale arises from the fact that the pupils were young boys, but even so it is not clear how even the older artist in the left foreground could retrieve his hat or how the bottle could be got down from the lower sash without the aid of the extra tall ladder conveniently propped against the bookcase.

4: DAVID ALLAN AND THE SCOTTISH INTERIOR
1765

In selecting the illustrations for this book it was decided to eschew portraits which incidentally introduced domestic details in favour of views of actual rooms. The artist, David Allan (1744–1796) showed an especial feeling for interior scenes. He received his early training at the Foulis Academy before departing for Italy to further his studies. From 1787 he was Master of the Board of Manufactures Drawing Academy in Edinburgh which had been founded in 1760 with the express purpose of equipping young apprentice to trades such as coach painting, paper-staining and textile manufacturing with the rudiments of design. Of all the early masters, Allan pursued this responsibility with the greatest seriousness and each year he produced designs of his own to help form his pupils' taste.

In his private capacity Allan was involved in interior design and Margaret Swain has shown how he helped Lady Mary Hogg with the lay-out of the appliqué embroidered panels which were installed in her Drawing Room at the new house of Newliston which Robert Adam designed. As early as 1765 when he is said to have drawn this portrait of the Shaw family [4a] Allan betrayed a lively interest in carefully observed domestic detail. However, there is little reason to believe that it shows an actual room at their country house, Schawpark, in spite of the seemingly realistic furniture. It is rather that the detail is introduced to convey information about the sitter. Indeed, the father's desire to be presented as a man of learning has been overstated to the extent of his appearing to ignore his numerous family. Even the table seems to be introduced to prop up yet more evidence of his interest in the arts and sciences, and the picture-hang is composed to give polish to the picture. Allan's conversation pieces such as 'The Connoisseurs' [4b], in the National Gallery of Scotland, necessarily introduce fashionable furnishings to promote his storyline. The

4a

· 19 ·

upper section of the large cabinet with its scrolled, broken pediment, fretwork and the raised bead on the doors with its concave corners is almost identical to an actual contemporary cabinet by William Brodie of 1786, now in the collections of the National Museums of Scotland. Although the underfurnished look and seat furniture are probably equally reliable exemplars of fashionable Edinburgh rooms, there is a strong sense in which the space is merely a stage-set. The composition is purely pictorial in its balance and is surprisingly devoid of architectural detail.

Allan was to prove immensely influential through his portrayal of genre scenes. As an illustrator of the poems of both Allan Ramsay and Burns, Allan had, of necessity, to portray everyday views from rural life but this activity seems to have particularly captured his imagination, doubtless because it gave him a splendid opportunity to add to the storyline with telling detail which led his biographer to describe him as 'The Scottish Hogarth'. Recently this aspect of his art has attracted the attention of scholars of Scottish vernacular architecture and many of the visual details which he recorded have been related to documentary descriptions of now vanished aspects of rural buildings [4c]. Through the work of Allan and his followers, Scotland is particularly rich in sources for the study of the vernacular interior.

4b

4c

5: A FURNITURE PLAN FOR KINNAIRD HOUSE, STIRLINGSHIRE
c.1770?

It would be difficult to imagine a rarer document than this schematic furniture plan for Kinnaird – nothing is known of the circumstances surrounding its production. Only the bedroom floor plan survives although it is clear from the room numbering that there was once a corresponding plan of the lower floor. It seems to be a record of where the furniture had been placed rather than a plan for its disposition. It confirms the standard eighteenth-century practice of disposing the furniture formally around the perimeter of the rooms, and not even in the Library are chairs drawn up to the central table. The rooms are named from their *en suite* textiles as the 'White Chintz' and 'Yellow Chintz' bedrooms and this seems to have been a standard practice. These names are also a reminder that printed linens were an important Scottish manufacture. The shaped toilet tables would have been dressed with flounced fabric covers. Among the many interesting details it is notable that the night tables are placed far away from the beds. It seems to be a modern practice to place them on either side of the bed now that they are used merely as bedside tables. Chairs are placed on either side of each bed and it may be that this was with a view to assisting the occupant mount the towering pile of mattresses.

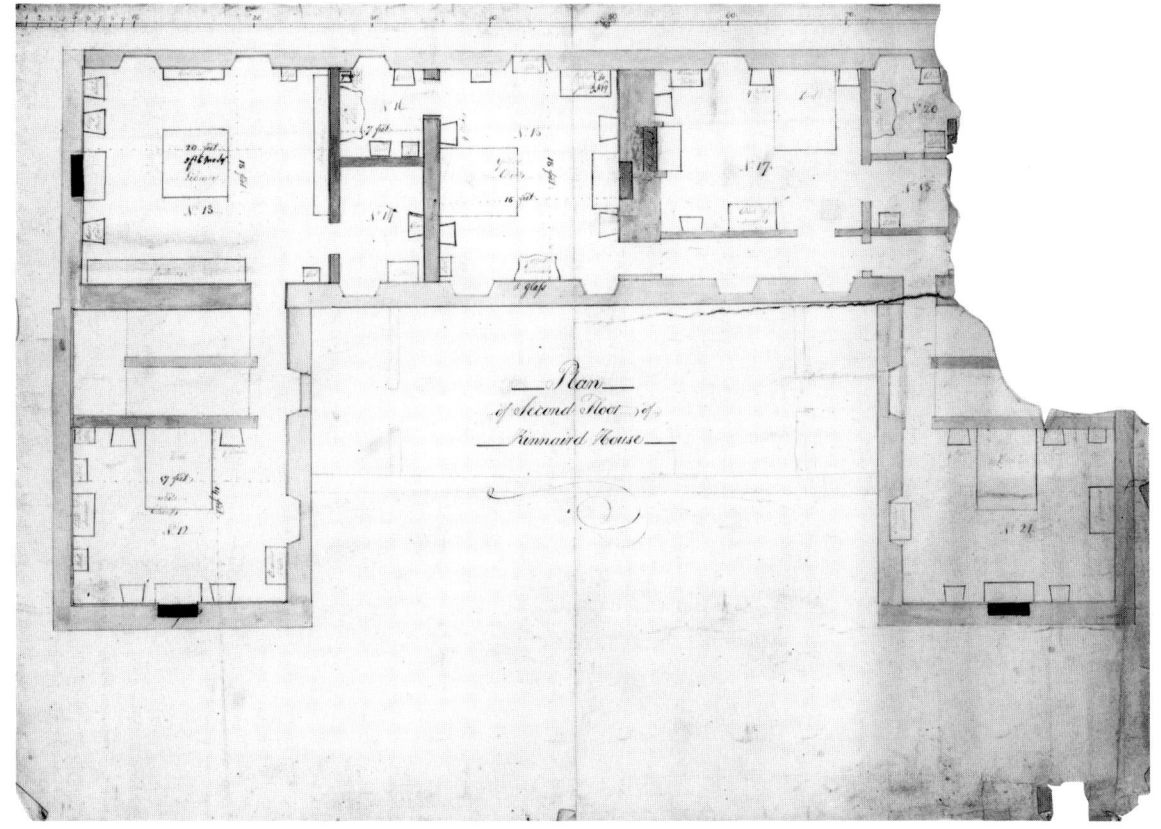

6: THE INSIDE OF A WEAVER'S COTTAGE IN ISLAY
1772

Thomas Pennant was something of a professional tourist, travelling in search of the curious with his personal artist, Moses Griffith, and publishing the results. His second *Tour in Scotland* of 1772 included a journey to the Hebrides and his report on the housing conditions of the people of Islay leaves no doubt as to his motivation in including this rare interior view. He was clearly appalled by the conditions they endured:

A set of people worn down by poverty: their habitations scenes of misery, made of loose stones; without chimneys, without doors, excepting the faggot opposed to the wind at one or other of the apertures, permitting the smoke to escape through the other, in order to prevent the pains of suffocation. The furniture perfectly corresponds: a pothook hangs from the middle of the roof, with a pot pendent over a grateless fire, filled with fare that may rather be called a permission to exist, than a support of vigorous life: the inmates lean, dusky and smoke dried. But my picture is not of this island only.

Griffith's view captures the squalor and even the dog looks thoroughly miserable,

7: THE ARTIST'S WORKSHOP WITH HIS TWO DAUGHTERS, ANN AND ELIZABETH, BY ALEXANDER NASMYTH
*c.*1800

In this sketch portrait of his daughters, Nasmyth has also captured a view of his workshop. The room was close to Alexander Nasmyth's heart because painting alone could not satisfy his inventive mind and many hours were passed in his workshop. His father had been an Edinburgh builder who particularly prided himself on the superior joinery of his houses. Nasmyth's most celebrated invention was his 'Sunday rivet' which earned its name because it was secured by compression rather than with hammering. Elizabeth was born in 1793 and Ann in 1798 so this view must date from *c.*1800. The workshop was situated in the attic and the elegant decorative painting with fictive panelling reflects the room's public character because the workshop was as much the resort of Edinburgh's fashionable world as the artist's studio. This kind of light ornamental painting was probably common in the New Town although few examples survive today. Traces of an elaborate scheme with birds holding garlands of flowers was recently discovered in an elegant Neo-Classical flat at the foot of Leith Walk.

Nasmyth's son, James, achieved fame as the inventor of the steam hammer. His career in engineering began with home made working models the parts for which were cast in a temporary casting shop on his bedroom hearth and finished on his father's workshop lathe.

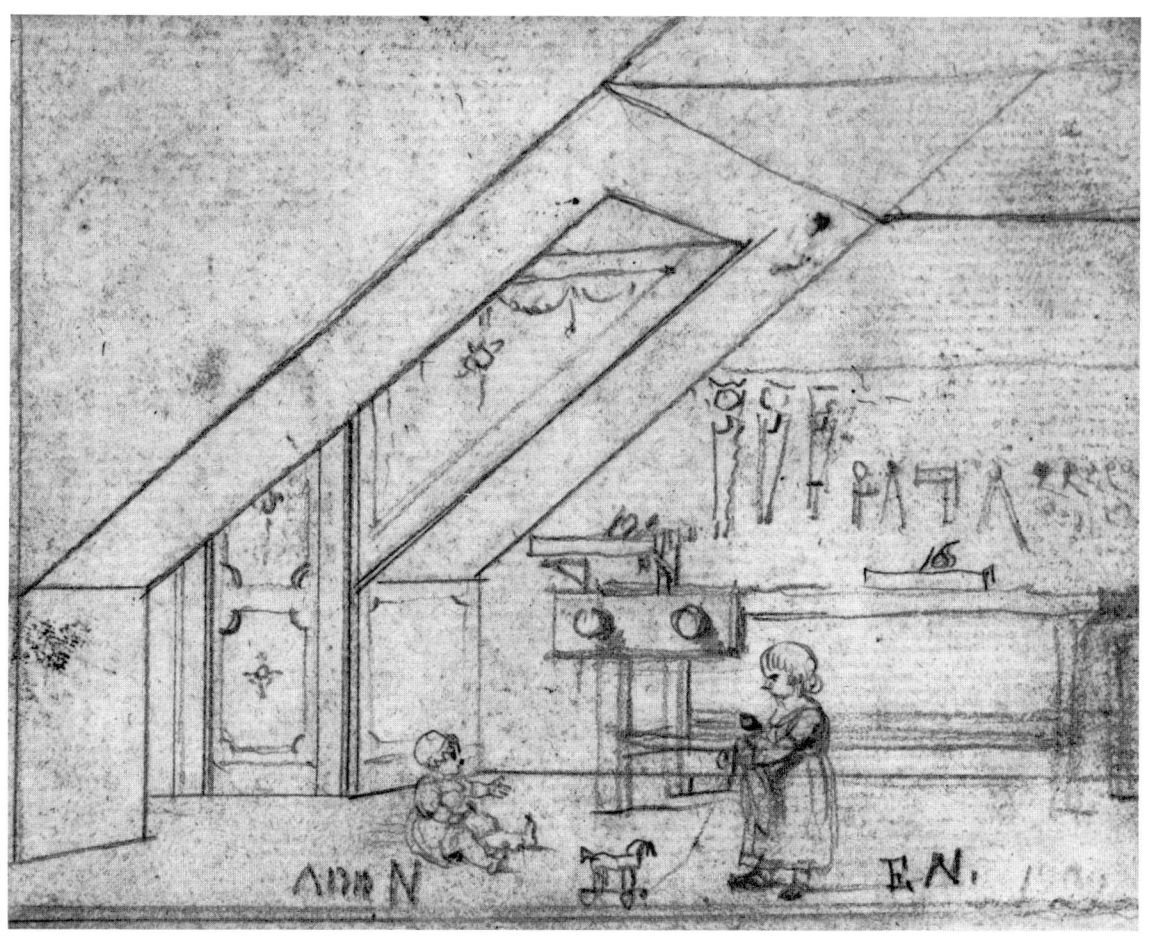

8: A SCHOOLBOY SKETCHES THE HERMITAGE AT DUNKELD
1806

This tiny, slight sketch appears to be the only visual record of one of the most exotic interiors in Scotland. The Hermitage at Dunkeld was begun in 1757 but refitted as 'Ossian's Hall' by the Fourth Duke of Atholl in 1783. This ornamental garden building was conceived as a viewpoint for the enjoyment of the adjacent waterfall and to enhance its effect the walls of the inner saloon were covered in mirrors and the windows were glazed with coloured glass. The decorations were completed with painted arabesques and 'Ossian's furniture' which had been manufactured in London. The oval-backed chairs may be those bearing lyres and japanned in green which are now displayed in the Derby Room at Blair Castle. Professor David Irwin has charted reactions to this room through successive published tours which reveal that initial delight gave way, under the influence of Picturesque taste, to a rejection of its contrived artificiality in the accounts of early nineteenth-century visitors. This sketch was made by the sixteen-year-old John Sime, who had a predilection for architecture, but it is interesting that he should have chosen to depict it in such a formal section rather than a sketch. It was perhaps just because it was such an unusual building that he included its furniture.

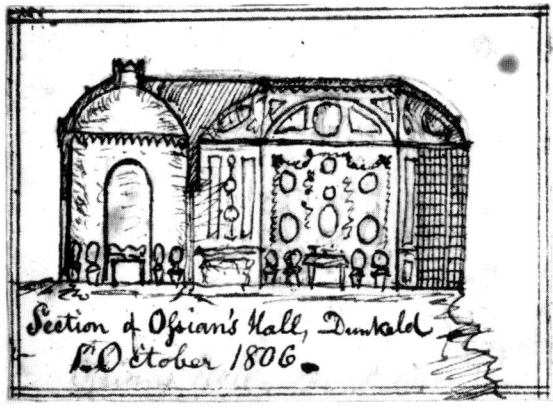

9: JOHN HARDEN'S SKETCHES OF HIS FATHER-IN-LAW'S HOUSE AT 28 QUEEN STREET, EDINBURGH
1807

John Harden was an amateur artist who married Jessy, daughter of an Edinburgh banker, Robert Allan. They subsequently set up home at Brathay Hall in the English Lake District and his watercolours of their life there have been frequently reproduced. The few portraits of the Allan family taken on visits to Queen Street are less familiar but have the distinction of being the earliest known views of Edinburgh New Town rooms. Although the drawings are primarily portrait studies, they have an immediacy which suggests that they were taken while he sat within the family circle. The drawing of Robert Allan was sent in 1807 to his daughter, Agnes, then resident in Bengal and she was also the recipient of Jessy's 'Journal' which was sent out in individual letters chronicling the events of Allan family life. Agnes valued the sketch highly as a likeness and because it portrayed her father in his favourite spot 'sitting at his writing Desk in the front Parlour of his House in Queen Street No 28 – the desk stood on a table between the windows and between them was a mirror, which beautifully reflected his fine countenance'. Another sketch shows that the table had a fitted writing-drawer. The second view shows the drawing room which was the setting for musical parties. The sculpture on its plinth appears in other views as do the set of oval backed arm chairs with their deep loose covers. Although the details of the interior are scant, they convey an impression of elegant simplicity which contrasts markedly with the extravagant opulence of the New Town during the 1820s. Interestingly, Jessy's diary contains a passage in 1802 which suggests that the younger generation were in tune with fashionable ideas:

> We then called on Aunt John and went with her to choose Drawing room chairs and Sophas at Young and Trotter. I was rallying her t'other day about having such shabby ones (for you must know I am beginning to observe these things a little more than formerly) when she told me she had been wishing for others a long time but grudged the expense of them: I told her that was no reason for her and promised to assist her in the choice of them when she pleased'.

9a

9b

10: MR AND MRS CAMPBELL WITH LADY MOLESWORTH
AND MISS BROWN IN THE DRAWING ROOM AT MIDFIELD COTTAGE,
LASSWADE, BY ALEXANDER CARSE
1807

This charming conversation piece has the distinction of being the first realistically detailed record of an actual room in Scottish art. Although domestic trappings had been a commonplace of earlier portraiture, there is a sense in which the enclosing walls were like stage back-cloths and the furnishings were carefully accumulated to reflect on the accomplishments of the sitters. Carse, by contrast, has set his small scale figures in the middle distance and there is a real sense of space defined by the prominent ceiling, rare in earlier interior scenes, and the curving back wall whose window allows the eye to travel out into the prospect of the Pentlands.

The picture seems to carry no message beyond the three sisters' pleasure in their own company in Mr Campbell's pretty house. The realism is confirmed by the existence of a pair of companion views showing the exterior of this ravishing thatched *cottage orné*, set in the beautiful Eskside villadom. Carse's interest in the minor details of daily life were to make him a successful, if never prosperous, exponent of genre subjects. The interior architecture is simple and reflects the under-stated taste of the late eighteenth century with its simple leaf cornice, well suited to a summer residence. The painting, however, records a moment of transition in taste and the severe architecture has been overlaid by a spirit of Picturesque informality most notable in the

plentiful use of textiles in the curtains framing the view and the fitted carpet. The chimneypiece, with its composition enrichments, is readily recognisable as the product of an as yet unidentified Edinburgh workshop. Although Carse's brushwork is insufficiently skilled to clarify many of the finer points, it appears to have been marbled to match the real marble slips surrounding the stove grate. The fitted carpet gives a cosy effect and appears to have a repeating geometric pattern suggesting that it was flatwoven. The unusual life-size statuary, the draperies and the scroll-end couches strike a Grecian attitude, and the introduction of this new Picturesque style did much to promote the breakdown of the old, essentially Roman, architectural formality. Carse seems to have got into a muddle in his depiction of the inner glass curtains and it is difficult to sort out just how they would work except that they appear to follow the curve of the bay. He certainly omitted a set of green-painted Venetian blinds which were included in his exterior view.

The most revolutionary departure from eighteenth-century norms is the way in which the furniture has been pulled away from the walls and there is a new diversification through the introduction of light multi-purpose tables which, like the octagonal worktable, could be moved around without the intervention of servants. Although to modern eyes the pictures and miniatures seem sparse, they have been carefully grouped to form a pattern above and opposite the chimneypiece. There is also a clutter of objects throughout the room creating a deliberately 'lived-in look' which may be realistic rather than solely serving Carse's pictorial purposes.

Such a relaxed atmosphere contrasts with more formal earlier Georgian habits. This is particularly underlined by the way in which the largest of the three semi-circular porcelain flower-containers has found a home on the cloth-covered centre table and is apparently permanently separated from its companions on the chimneypiece where all three belong. The pile of books on the chimneypiece, the most important item and focal point of an early Georgian interior, would have seemed shockingly casual to a former generation even in a villa drawing room.

John Sime's precocious study of the Hermitage at Dunkeld has already been illustrated (8) and the origin of this exceptionally rare record also lies in a student architect's essay. Sime has attempted to replan his family's cramped living space in their tenement flat in Fairbairn's Land of Edinburgh's Lawnmarket. His modish 'after' solution with its elegant curved walls is eclipsed in interest, however, by the information conveyed by his 'before' drawing. In addition to naming the functions of the spaces, Sime shows the furniture plan. The parlour is the only public room but it has a bed in its closet behind folding doors. Another bed closet was appropriately called the 'Dark Room', a name that recurs in inventories. The kitchen has a folding bed and this seems to have been a common and necessary item of furniture. The back bedroom probably also functioned as a reception room and has the best bed and the important sounding 'Escritoire'. The furniture is both ranged round the walls and its placing, particularly the chairs, follows formal patterns. The houses of the New Town must have seemed palaces by comparison for people accustomed to living at such close quarters with each other.

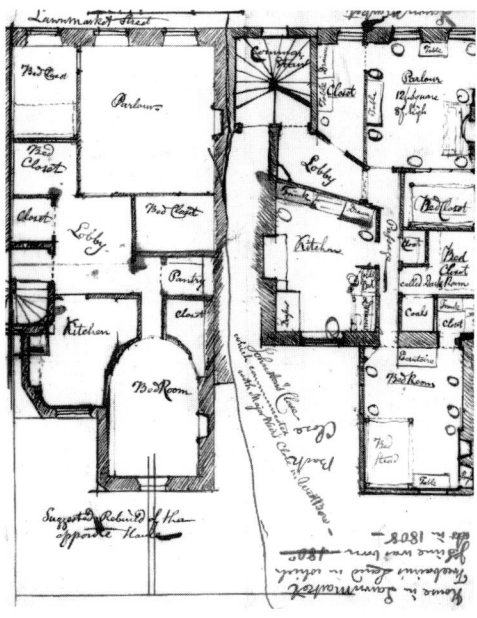

12a

12b

12: JAMES GILLESPIE GRAHAM'S PROPOSAL
FOR A SUITE OF DRAWING ROOMS AT SPRINGWOOD PARK, KELSO
c.1822

It is very intriguing that the earliest drawings to depict the design of a room in perspective, superseding the eighteenth-century section, should have been introduced in Scotland just at the moment when artists like Carse began to draw actual rooms. It is significant that these extremely elaborate perspective presentation drawings should have been produced in the office of the architect, James Gillespie Graham, who, of all the early nineteenth-century members of his profession, seems to have had the greatest feeling for interiors. The drawings would have been helpful in explaining to his patron at Springwood Park (probably Sir John James Scott-Douglas) his novel Picturesque scheme, whereby the public rooms would be opened up into a dramatic suite of rooms culminating in the vista through a conservatory.

The simplicity of the Grecian architectural detail is complemented by the sumptuous, and equally Grecian in inspiration, draperies with their continued valances supported by massive gilded poles. A realistic effect is promoted by the inclusion of carpets, chimney-ornaments and fire-irons, but the omission of the furniture harks back to earlier conventions in architectural drawing. The exceptions are the pairs of torchères placed inside the columnar screen and under the arch. It is interesting that Gillespie Graham produced finished elevations for them showing their ornaments in detail. The perspective was to become of great importance for depicting exteriors, as architectural competitions proliferated and it was common for architects to commission artists to execute their entries.

13: TWO GOTHIC GALLERIES
AT SCONE PALACE AND KINFAUNS CASTLE
1827–8

Such is the paucity of early views of Scottish interiors that this painting of the Gallery at Scone of *c.*1827 by Robert Gibb, described by John Cornforth as 'one of the clearest records that I know', and the inclusion of a similar and equally rare view of the Gallery at nearby Kinfauns in the second series of J. P. Neale's *Views of the Seats* could not be a coincidence. The answer lies in the very active patronage of Lord Gray at Kinfauns, who had employed Sir Robert Smirke to rebuild the castle in a medieval style, stressing the great antiquity of the family. The range of Lord Gray's interests is reflected by the presence of a 'Laboratory' among his private apartments. The family's ancient possessions were shown off in their new setting by the Earl who was also an active collector and patron of living artists. His achievements in these fields are recorded in the two sumptuous catalogues to both the library and the pictures that were produced by D. Morison on the Castle's own printing press. Their elaborate decorative borders were deliberately intended to recall medieval illuminations. The Library Catalogue of 1828 has a series of standard borders, printed in red, reflecting the subject matter of the divisions into which the books had been arranged. The list of books was overprinted in the blank central rectan-

gles left for this purpose but, in an additional elaboration, further illustrations reflecting the contents of particular books diversify the blocks of text so that Slezer's *Theatrum Scotiae*, for instance, is accompanied by a view of Falkland Palace. The Picture Catalogue of 1833 is a refinement on its predecessor with notes by Francis Grant and its illuminations have applied watercolour highlights in the presentation copy from Hamilton Palace that is now in the Victoria and Albert Museum. The key to Neale's view of the Gallery is provided in the description of a painting of a waterfall by Robert Gibb:

The young artist was bred to the profession of house painting, but his zeal to excel as an artist induced him to leave this occupation, and commence his career in Edinburgh as a landscape painter, without money or patronage. In this situation he was recommended to Lord Gray, who got him admitted to the Academy of the Royal Institution. His Lordship has since employed him to paint, several pictures, the best of which is executed with much delicacy and truth. It has been engraved for Neale's Views. Mr Gibb is at present, 1827, following his profession in Edinburgh.

In the description of the Gallery painting itself, which is

sadly now lost, Grant writes:

> *This picture is finished with great delicacy and the detail is made out with wonderful accuracy, the marbles, bronzes, cabinets, vases etc.are beautifully and faithfully delineated. The artist was occupied nearly three months in painting this picture which is highly creditable to his talents and industry.*

The severe Neo-Classical outline style of Neale's engraving cannot recapture the liveliness of the original painting. The Gallery was described as being 'eighty two feet in length, from which the principal rooms enter. In the centre is a large, three-sided projection each compartment occupied by a handsome window of stained glass'. The Gallery was furnished in antiquarian style with old cabinets and chairs to complement its Gothic architecture but it also incorporated several more recent objects including a clock, just visible on the far right, reputed to have belonged to Marie Antoinette, while 'the huge marble vase set on a pedestal' had been made 'by the order of Empress Josephine and bought by Lord Gray at Naples'. The Earl's patronage extended to Neale himself because the 1932 sale catalogue of the Library included as 'Lot 212 Neale J. P. Seventy-six original drawings of seats in Scotland, presented to Francis Lord Gray by the artist'. In his text Neale is effusive in his description of his patron's merits.

Inspired by the Gibb view of the Gallery, Morison went on to produce an almost identical view of his own, and others of the Ante Room, the Drawing Room and the Library for inclusion in the Catalogue of Pictures. Although they have considerable charm, they rather tend to confirm the high contemporary repute in which Gibb's abilities were held. The largest contract for the furnishings went to the London firm of Dowbiggin who were thus presumably responsible for the Gothic style furniture harmonising with the architecture shown in Morison's survey.

Drawn by J.P.Neale.   Engraved by R.Sands. *13a*

Presumably Lord Mansfield at neighbouring Scone Palace saw the Gibb painting of the Kinfauns Gallery and was inspired, or encouraged by Lord Gray, to ask the artist to perform a similar service. The Scone painting, however, is larger than the missing Kinfauns picture the measurements of which were only one foot seven inches by one foot. The grandeur of the Scone Gallery reflected its medieval origins and it was almost the only element of the plan of medieval Scone to be carried through to the modern Palace when it was rebuilt to the designs of William Atkinson in the Gothic style from 1802. Although later accounts fondly wished to believe that details of the room were ancient it is clear that every element was designed by Atkinson and, on account of its great length and run of vaulting, it is one of the most elaborate of all early Gothic revival rooms in Scotland. Its impact and degree of conviction originally depended very much on the skills of the house-painter who transformed the gimcrack white plaster vaults and shafts into

a realistic impression of jointed and polished ashlars. Although Gibb, who had sufficient problems of perspective to tackle, not unnaturally chose to omit this detail, the fictive jointing is recorded in old photographs. The house-painter at Scone in 1816 was no less than the young David Roberts, who after having completed his apprenticeship with Gavin Beugo of Edinburgh, found employment with 'Mr Conway of London' who had won the painting contract. Although the Scone Gallery was used to display a range of art objects like that at Kinfauns, it is much more of a room in its own right and has comfortable modern seat furniture in addition to antiques. The centre of the Gallery is lined with ottomans which would have been useful during organ recitals. The Kinfauns Gallery functioned primarily as an access corridor and its practical drugget strip down the centre of the bare boards contrasts with the sumptuous parquet at Scone.

13b

13c

13d

13e

14: DOWBIGGIN'S FURNITURE PLAN FOR THE DRAWING ROOM AT SALTOUN HALL
c.1822

Saltoun Hall was transformed by substantial additions in the Gothic style by William Burn from 1818–22. This design is by the London cabinet-maker and upholsterer, Thomas Dowbiggin, and shows his proposal for fitting up the Drawing Room. Although the architecture is rendered schematically, a hybrid mixture of section, plan and perspective sketches is used to convey all the necessary information about the design and disposition of the furniture in a very economical manner. The drawing shows that the old formal disposition of the furniture around the perimeter of the room had given way to a new fashion for apparent informality with a major cluster concentrated round a centre table in front of the fire with subsidiary groups round the centre and corner ottomans. This enabled individual members of the family or their guests to pursue particular interests while the main party occupied the centre table. As the necessity for the plan suggests, this apparently informality had its own structure. Many wealthy landowners ordered their drawing room furniture from London, with Scottish firms supplying the minor bedroom quarters and dining rooms. Dowbiggin himself had a number of Scottish clients. Although Edinburgh's largest firm, Trotter, could supply all that was required in a country house by the 1820s, it became fashionable during the 1830s and 1840s to order drawing-room furniture from Paris, and this was the case at Burn's House of Falkland and David Hamilton's Lennox Castle. Curiously, Trotter does not seem to have produced this kind of drawing and when a client in Ireland requested designs they were politely informed that Trotter's customers usually visited the Edinburgh wareroom at 8 Princes Street in person. There was no call for drawings because examples of the furniture supplied by the firm were exhibited. When the client insisted on drawings, Trotter was forced to supply a sketch plan for the disposition of the drawing room whose crudity stands in marked contrast to Dowbiggin's suave design.

Facing: 14

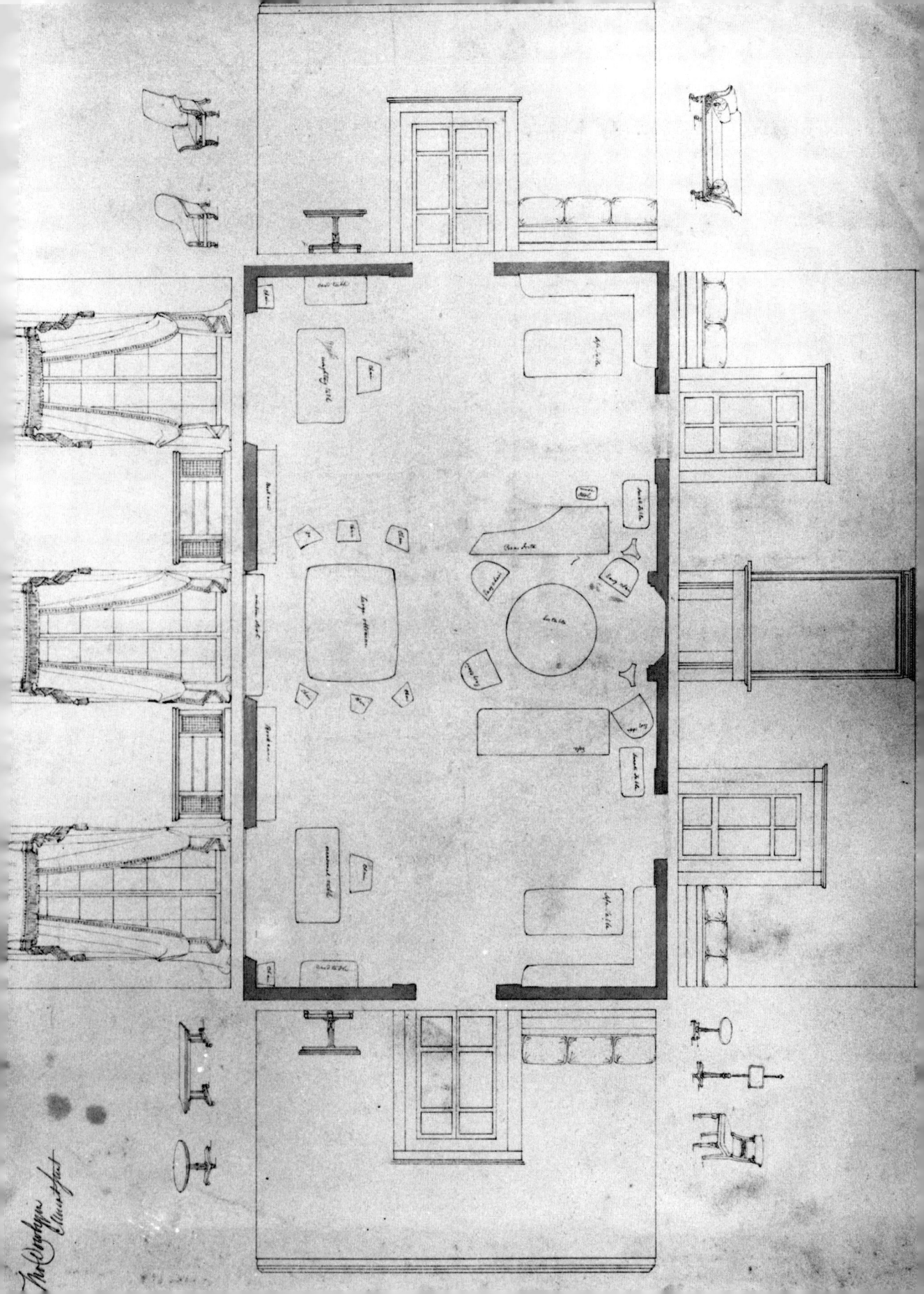

Although the *Historical and Descriptive Account of the Palace and Chapel-Royal of Holyroodhouse* published in 1826 not unnaturally concentrated on the colourful early history of the Palace, the excitement engendered by George IV's State Visit to Scotland in 1822 was still sufficiently fresh to inspire the inclusion of this engraving of the 'State Room'. Its smart modernity was out of character with the ancient Palace but was the result of the peculiar arrangements that prevailed for the King's brief visit. The derelict condition of Holyrood made it impractical for the King, with his luxurious tastes, to reside there and he was actually accommodated among the modern comforts of Dalkeith Palace, the seat of the Duke of Buccleuch. Holyrood's historical importance, however, merited its temporary resuscitation for a levee and reception, but the Treasury were not prepared to allow more than a minimal sum towards this.

Perhaps because it only came to life for a few hours, and the King was thus as much a visitor as his subjects, he was given exclusive use of the Great Stair while they entered the Royal Apartment by the Picture Gallery staircase. This was the very reverse of the usage that Charles II and his architect, Sir William Bruce, had so carefully intended for their sumptuously decorated chain of Baroque state apartments. The Throne Room was therefore rather eccentrically established in what had been planned as the outer Guard Chamber – but it was perhaps equally likely that nobody could remember how the suite was meant to function because of royalty's long absence from Scotland. Because it was intended as the humblest room in the apartment, it had never received a splendid fretwork ceiling or panelling like the adjoining rooms. Its only ornament was a bolection-moulded marble fire surround. The lack of decorations may have been seen as a positive asset, however, because it allowed for a free expression of late-Georgian taste. A new cornice in Neoclassical style was installed. The walls were hung with crimson cloth by William Trotter, the leading furniture maker in Edinburgh who must also have been responsible for the 'gorgeous'

continued curtain draperies with their massive tassels and the very architectural chimney-glass. This finery was to some extent borrowed because the centre-piece, the Throne itself, was second-hand. It had been originally commissioned by Queen Charlotte for her saloon at Buckingham House. After the Queen's death in 1818, her son began to rebuild her house, and the throne, having become surplus to requirements, was despatched to lend a note of metropolitan glitter to dowdy Holyrood at a minimal cost. The King's cipher was substituted for his mother's on the velvet draperies but the wreath of oak leaves, more suitable for an English palace remained.

The author of the text accompanying the plate noted that it had 'but one fault (with some a very important one) that the Unicorn is placed on the wrong side for a state room in Scotland'. The crimson velvet on the Throne and its canopy with the crimson cloth on the walls provided a splendid foil for the lavish gilding of all the mouldings. Even the mouldings on the doors were gilt and it looks as though the fillets were overlaid on cloth on the principle of the more familiar draught-excluding baize doors. Although the miniaturised figures help to increase the apparent scale of the room, the bareness is accurate enough because the resplendent furniture supplied for the occasion by Trotter had merely been hired and it left the Palace shortly after the King.

The author made a not wholly convincing but valiant attempt to wed this modern elegance to the Palace's past glories on the grounds that its furnishings 'convey at once an idea of the internal decoration of Royal dwellings, and more particularly the exhibition of it during the residence of ancient Scottish Monarchs in this Palace'.

David Allan's interest in genre scenes was developed by later generations of Scottish artists of whom the most outstandingly successful was Sir David Wilkie. Although Allan had introduced authentic details to extend his storyline, nineteenth-century artists increasingly composed their paintings from sketches taken directly from actual vernacular buildings, in the pursuit of verisimilitude. These drawings are of great value today for the study of Scotland's rural architecture. As Dr Errington predicted in 1985:

The drawings such as Wilkie made from 1817 are for most of the century the only satisfactory evidence – because far more specific than even the most detailed written account – of the interiors of rural cottages, describing not only what was inside these houses but exactly where it was. It seems entirely possible that in the drawings of Wilkie and his followers there is a resource that the social and architectural historians have scarcely begun to exploit or appreciate, but however true that may be, Wilkie's activities in this line can only be properly understood in relation to the Scottish conservation or revival movement in literature of the early nineteenth century.

16a

Walter Geikie (1795–1837) was a highly original artist who was deaf and dumb and who enjoyed considerable popularity through his character studies. The National Gallery of Scotland possesses a fascinating sketchbook of his studies of rural houses which presumably served as a quarry for the composition of synthetic genre scenes. Dr Duncan Macmillan first drew attention to it as a source and the drawing illustrated here is the only one to bear a positive identification. Cousland is a village in Midlothian and this sketch is replete with carefully observed detail about the way such houses were used with its line of box beds with chests or kists in front of them and furniture derived from fashionable patterns. Taken together, and in comparison to the Weaver's Cottage on Islay [6], they project an impression of prosperity rather than the breadline. Although superficially similar, the purpose of the third drawing by Sir William Allan was to preserve a record of this particular farmhouse because Mossgiel had been rented from 1784–8 by Robert Burns. The sketch comes from the extensive biographical collection assembled by W. F. Watson, an Edinburgh bookseller, which was left to the National Gallery of Scotland. His drawings were elaborately arranged in portfolios:

> to display a Man's likeness, Birthplace, and Tomb; his Writing, Drawing, or Etching; his Calling Card, Book-plate, or Coat of Arms; the Advertisement of his Works; the proposal for Publishing, or Title Page of his Book; the intimation of his Death, or invitation to his Funeral, or, it may be, ticket for his Trial or Speech at his Execution.

Both Burns and Scott were particular enthusiasms and it is fascinating to see how the artists Watson employed or

persuaded to make these records, drew the rooms, where, say, Scott met Burns at Sciennes House [16d], exactly as they existed, untroubled by their later anachronisms, which were to become such a worry to antiquarian illustrators.

16d

16c

17a

Sir Walter Scott's phenomenal popularity is reflected in the plethora of illustrations of his beloved Abbotsford. Curiously, however, none of the interior views seem to have been made during Scott's lifetime with the exception of this set, the purpose of which was described by Scott's son-in-law and biographer, J. G. Lockhart. As Scott's fatal illness progressed during the final summer at Abbotsford of 1832, Lockhart records in his *Life of Sir Walter Scott*:

> *Perceiving, towards the close of August, that the end was near, and thinking it very likely that Abbotsford might soon undergo many changes and myself, at all events, never see it again, I felt a desire to have some image preserved of the interior apartments, as occupied by the founder, and invited from Edinburgh for that purpose Sir Walter's dear friend, William Allan – whose presence I well knew, would even under the circumstances of that time be nowise troublesome to any of the family but the contrary in all respects. Mr Allan willing, complied, and executed a beautiful series of drawings.*

In fact, so successfully did Lockhart resolve the Scott family's financial problems after Sir Walter's death that the house has been maintained as Scott's memorial and his biographer would find few changes today beyond the loss of carpets and textiles which have worn out. The pressure of tourists (see [17a], by John Ewbank) almost made Abbotsford impossible to live in for his descendants and they all but gave up, in 1853 commissioning the architect, William Burn, to add a new private entrance on the opposite side of the house from the tourist route.

Although Scott had built for his pleasure alone, few shrines can be so visually rewarding to literary disciples. In planning his home, Scott brought the same powerful imagination to bear that had conceived his poetry and novels.

Abbotsford has a strong theatrical element that has both delighted and exasperated visitors, according to their taste, for the last one hundred and fifty years. It is very much a villa expressing Scott's personal whims and fancies rather than a true country house designed to serve as the long-term seat of a family.

Scott's early legal career confined him to Edinburgh but he, in common with many fellow citizens, had rented a variety of properties as summer villas as his means expanded. In 1811, his lease of Ashestiel expired and he decided to purchase Abbotsford which, although it occupied a fine situation on a stretch of the Tweed near Melrose, was really a farmhouse. The gradual replacement of the old house proceeded in proportion to the profits from his literary successes. Scott had strong views on both architecture and decoration but his delight in building seems to have been heightened by long discussions with friends, who helped to dare him into further extravagances. If William Atkinson, the architect, who had been a pupil of James Wyatt, was a key figure at Abbotsford in turning the ideas into reality, his position was very much that of executant architect and Scott put equal reliance on a circle of friends and craftsmen.

The acquisition of a permanent home meant that the rapidly growing collection of antiquities in his Edinburgh house at 39 Castle Street could be more appropriately displayed in rooms at Abbotsford which were especially designed to show to advantage his collection of armour and the relics of famous Scots. The most innovatory feature of the new house was this self-consciously Scottish character and not only were details of historic buildings faithfully copied but a quantity of ancient stonework and carving was physically incorporated, as were a large series of casts of medieval carving from such major monuments as Melrose Abbey and Roslin Chapel. Such an idiosyncratic approach would have been hindered by the employment of an architect with decided views and tastes and this perhaps also explains why he relished working with malleable local craftsmen like his builders, the Smiths of Darnick, rather than fashionable Edinburgh firms. An insight into Scott's methods is provided by his selection of David Ramsay Hay, who was to prove one of Scott's most inspired discoveries. Scott may have known Hay's mother, Rebecca Carmichael, who was a minor Edinburgh poetess. After the early death of his father, Hay was found a position in the printing trade, but after

displaying a greater interest in artistic pursuits, he was apprenticed to a house-painter which was then a conventional training for a future artistic career. Scott not only recommended Hay for a place in the Academy of the Board of Trustees but had also commissioned from him a portrait of the stray cat, Heinze, who had been Scott's constant companion in his study at Castle Street during his early compositions. When this painting was delivered to his patron, Hay received the following advice:

I have thought for some time, that were young men who have a genius for painting, and who are not possessed of sufficient patrimony to enable them to follow such a course of study as alone can raise them in the fine arts, to endeavour to improve those professions in which a taste for painting is required, it would be a more lucrative field for their exertion. I know no profession that stands more in need of this than that to which you have been bred, and if you

17b

· 39 ·

follow my advice, you will apply yourself to its improvement, instead of struggling with the difficulties that you must meet in following the higher walks of art.

As an additional inducement Hay was offered the decoration of Abbotsford as his first commission. There was an element of enlightened self-interest in Scott's patronage because in the young Hay he had a house-painter who was exceptionally anxious to please.

The period of Hay's apprenticeship had seen a revolution in the trade brought about by the introduction of a taste for elaborate decorative painting effects, imitating woods and marbles with such scientific accuracy as to deceive the eye. These skills were especially important in Gothic revival architecture and Hay's talents were given full rein in Abbotsford's rooms where the new fashions were enthusiastically promoted in opposition to the colour washes and white woodwork of Neo-Classical decoration. Lockhart provides an illuminating commentary on Scott's taste:

In the painting of his interior, too, Sir Walter personally directed everything. He abominated the common-place daubing of walls, panels, doors, and window boards, with coats of white blue, or grey, and thought that sparklings and edgings of gilding only made their baldness and poverty more noticeable. He desired to have about him, wherever he could manage it, rich, though not gaudy, hangings, or substantial old-fashioned wainscot-work, with no ornament but that of carving; and where the wood was to be painted at all, it was done in strict imitation of oak or cedar. Except in the drawing-room which he abandoned to Lady Scott's taste, all the roofs were in appearance of antique carved oak, relieved by coats of arms duly blazoned at the intersections of beams, and, resting on cornices to the eye of the same material but really composed of casts in plaster of Paris, after the foliage, the flowers, the grotesque monsters and dwarfs, and sometimes the beautiful heads of nuns and confessors, on which he had doted from infancy among the cloisters of Melrose and Roslin.

Hay responded to his patron's deep interest in decoration with inspired resourcefulness. The Entrance Hall incorporated a quantity of carved oak woodwork from

17

William Allan fecit
Edinburgh 1844

17d

Dunfermline Abbey but gave rise to problems. Hay wrote:

> The pulpit was, if I recollect rightly, circular, and some other difficulties arose during the progress of the carpenter's work, in its application to the wall of the entrance-hall. A further supply was therefore required, and upon this subject Sir Walter wrote to me from Abbotsford, asking me if I knew of anything of the kind in Edinburgh that could be purchased at moderate price. At that time there were no shops in Edinburgh, such as those where old carvings can now be so easily obtained – for I believe Sir Walter Scott's adoption of these articles as a decoration, gave the first impulse to that rage for them which has since existed, and which is now so well responded to by all who deal in other antiquities. This letter brought to my recollection that at the door of a house that stood (and still stands) in a wood-yard at the foot of Warriston's close in the High Street, there was a white painted porch with carved panels, the figures upon which used, long before, to be a subject of admiration to me and other boys attending a school in the neighbourhood. I therefore called upon the owner and obtained permission to examine it. Upon doing so, I found it was made of oak, and the figures in the panels were allegorical of the cardinal virtues etc. The owner of these panels … agreed to let me have those in his possession for as much money as would cover the expense of putting up a new porch to his house.

The bill for a new cast iron porch is preserved with that for the panels thus purchased by Hay at Abbotsford. The carvings provided Hay with his 'key' to the decoration and:

> In directing the painting of this apartment, Sir Walter desired that it should all be done in imitation of oak ; not like wood-work newly fitted-up, but to resemble the old oak carvings as much as possible. Neither would he allow it to appear like old oak newly varnished, as he had strictly forbid the varnishing of the old oak itself. He said, if it were possible, he should like the whole to appear somewhat weather-beaten and faded, as if it had stood untouched for many years. The doors, architraves, and part of the wainscoting were fitted up with new oak, and this he also ordered to be toned down to match the old carvings.

These effects are much closer to stage scenery than traditional decorative practice but Hay's account reveals the extent of Scott's personal involvement in directing the work so that according to Hay, Abbotsford 'remains to this day not the least interesting and remarkable creation of his wonderful mind'.

Scott's deep interest in decoration was to bear important fruit through Hay's subsequent career and it was Scott who introduced his protégé to William Nicholson, the artist, and his brother George, whose capital enabled them to set up Nicholson and Hay, becoming the capital's leading decorators until 1828 when, following a quarrel over the Nicholsons' commercial attitude to the business, Hay set up on his own.

The record drawings of Abbotsford which Allan executed for Lockhart show the main rooms of the final and largest addition which Scott made to Abbotsford and their scale reflects his success before financial disaster overtook him. The new rooms were ready for Hay's painting in 1823 as the accounts show. A later watercolour gives a better impression of the liveliness of the Hall with its stained glass and highly-polished armour than do Allan's monochrome drawings, but the latter have the interest of revealing the furniture arrangement during Scott's lifetime. The big library with its richly-ornamented ceiling, cedar book cases and sumptuous furnishings like the carved Italian chairs in the bay which were presented by Scott's publisher Archibald Constable, contrasts with the workmanlike appearance of the study where Scott actually wrote his books. The study desk, as Clive Wainwright who has painstakingly reconstructed the history of the entire collection records, was a copy ordered from Gillow's of a desk originally made for Scott's friend, John Morrit of Rokeby and had originally stood in the study at 39 Castle Street.

This dramatic oblique view by James Giles is undoubtedly the most considerable work of art illustrated in this book and presents an ambitious study of light and shade. The success of the painting may reflect the artist's intimacy with his patron, Lord Aberdeen, the future Prime Minister. Giles had been born in Aberdeen in 1801, and was introduced to Lord Aberdeen in 1830 by another of his local patrons, Mr Gordon of Fyvie. Giles subsequently spent up to three months each summer at Haddo collaborating with the Earl in his antiquarian pursuits and in the design of a landscape garden. Giles' illustrations for a projected book on the castles of Aberdeenshire survive at the house. Lord Aberdeen's passion for the improvement of his estate is reflected in his reputed planting of fourteen million trees. Neither his first nor his second wife spent much time at Haddo and perhaps for this reason the house was to take second place to the park and Lord Aberdeen 'was wont to say that he must leave the overhauling of the *inside* of the house to his successor – he had devoted himself entirely to the transformation of the 1700 acres of policies, from the bare neglected state in which he found them into a demesne of varied beauty and charm'. Giles' view confirms this and perhaps understandably gives unusual prominence, in an interior, to the prospect out across

the parkland. There seem to have been no structural changes to the very architectural panelled room which William Adam had designed in the 1730s as the Great Dining Room of his new Haddo House. The improvements have been limited to cosmetic decoration to bring the room into line with modern taste. The panelling has been oak grained and the plaster cove tinted to harmonise. The heraldic decorations may be the work of Giles himself. The textiles are in a fashionable and scientific colour scheme where crimson has been deliberately contrasted with olive green. This has been followed through in the contrast binding of the curtains, the strip carpet made up to create a diagonal dropped pattern and the table and chair covers. The arrangement of the furniture is unusually formal for the period but this, like the extreme elegance of the caned armchairs, may reflect the Hellenic tastes of the Earl who had published a study of Greek Art and architecture after his return from his travels there.

This may be a posthumous portrait of Lady Aberdeen who died in 1833. The painting is an interesting illustration of firescreens in use, protecting the ladies' complexions from the heat of the fire. Giles has signed and dated his view in the inscription on the letter casually propped on the writing table in the foreground.

Mary Queen of Scots' Bedchamber [19c] at Holyrood was the most famous room in Scotland and this status is confirmed by its scoring the largest number of record drawings, engravings and lithographs. The finest views are these large lithographs by Swarbreck of 1838 which are also the earliest. Swarbreck takes advantage of the new medium to present an exceptionally detailed and apparently truthful record without exaggeration, down to the eccentric vertical, rather than horizontal, placing of the fenders. The latter is a reminder that the Bedchamber represented a new type of room the sole function of which was to be inspected by tourists and thus it necessarily stood beyond the reach of fashionable norms and conventional housekeeping standards. The Bedchamber's tenacious hold on popular taste arose not only from its proving exceptionally visually rewarding in matching up to the expectations of tourists but it also came with a story of operatic intensity – the brutal murder of David Rizzio. In addition the abandoned Palace could provide a rallying point for incipient romantic nationalism as James Ballantine's poem shows:

Is there a Scot but feels his heart
Pierced to the core by sorrow's dart
*   While gazing sadly on*
These ancient mouldering Abbey walls
These lone deserted Palace Halls
*   That vacant kingless throne.*

The extraordinary feature of the rooms was that their decorations and contents had accrued by accident. If a stage designer working to a brief by Mrs Radcliffe, or perhaps rather more appropriately Sir Walter Scott, had been asked to devise a bedroom for the Martyred Queen, they could scarcely have contrived a more atmospheric setting than that created by the cumulative effect of the ancient, armorial ceiling, the rose damask four poster, the requisite yardage of curious old tapestry and the fantastic tattered hangings of the Royal Closet [19b]. In reality their development arose because the sixteenth-century tower had been the only part of the

19a

19b

Palace to come through the destruction of the Civil Wars unscathed. In Charles II's reconstruction it formed the matrix of the new classical Palace and was refitted to form the Queen's Apartment but, because in practice neither sovereign or consort ever resided in the building, these rooms were appropriated by the Duke of Hamilton who claimed this privilege as Hereditary Keeper. The Hamiltons refurnished the newly repanelled and plastered rooms in princely style with magnificent beds and seat furniture in cut velvet and damask with elaborate fringes. During the 1740s the Duke of Hamilton employed William Adam to modernize the first floor rooms, and his Duchess was given a fashionable new bed. Because of their historic interest as the oldest rooms in the Palace the Hamilton apartments naturally attracted visitors. In 1760 the Duchess of Northumberland recorded in her diary:

I went also to see Mary Queen of Scots' Bedchamber (a very small one it is) from whence David Rizzio was drag'd out and stab'd in the ante room where is some of his Blood which they can't get wash'd out.

As the visitors multiplied it seems that the second floor rooms, which were in less constant use, were increasingly made over to tourism. Showing the rooms became an important duty and profitable perquisite of the Duke's housekeeper. The abandoned Duchess's bed of the 1680s took on a major role in the drama as the resting place of Mary Queen of Scots. Its great beauty and tattered condition made it well fitted for such stardom as, in Sir Walter Scott's words, 'the couch of the Rose of Scotland'. The other Baroque lumber supplied an able supporting cast and, from time to time, further relics accrued.

Something of the character of a tour of the apartments can be gleaned from the many editions of the guide-book which were available. That of 1818 states:

In the floor above are Queen Mary's apartments, in which her own bed, and many articles of furniture still remain. The bed is of crimson damask, bordered with green stalk tassels and fringes, and now almost in tatters. The cornice of the bed is of open figured work in the present taste, but more light in the execution than any modern one... The armour of Henry Darnley and James VI is shewn in the room from which Rizzio was dragged out to be murdered... In this suite of apartments there are some very good pictures... The furniture is said to be the same used in the time of Queen Mary. Chairs covered with crimson velvet, and highly ornamented with coronets upon the backs, etc.

Because the housekeeper was tipped for her services it was perhaps only natural that each object should, be woven into an ever-improving storyline which had been tried and tested through visitors' reactions. In the primitive state of furniture history, these housekeeper's tales may have given little concern but, one suspects, from time to time she must have had a tough time with the smattering of more learned tourists who were able to bring the attuned eye of the antiquarian to these surroundings and there is a growing unease in the published accounts of reconciling the eye with the mind. In his commentary to *Scotland Delineated*, John Parker Lawson MA, poured scorn on the ensemble:

In the north-west towers are Queen Mary's Apartments and those of the Duke of Hamilton. The former containing furniture of no greater antiquity than the time of Charles I. In the west front of the tower is the Queen's bedchamber, the walls covered with tapestry, and a very decayed bed is shown as that on which Mary reposed. The Queen's reputed dressing-room in the south-west turret is entered from this room, and also the closet in the north-west turret from which Riccio was dragged in the presence of Mary to be inhumanly murdered. In the Queen's Presence-chamber, as it is called, are shown several articles, some of them housewifery, alleged to have belonged to Queen Mary and Lord Darnley, particularly the pretended boots, lance, and iron breast-plate of the latter, the whole of which are evidently spurious. This apartment also contains a profusion of pictures and prints, chiefly of the seventeenth century, of no great merit.

Such debunking, however, had little effect on the room's popularity and it is amusing to note that Parker's pompous text accompanied a spirited illustration by the artist, George Cattermole, showing moment of the abduction

Overleaf: 19c

in front of the same offending bed. Antiquarian draughtsmen now had problems with their views but although R. W. Billings omitted a degree of clutter [24g], it is interesting to see in the accompanying text, which was supplied by John Hill Burton, the caution of the historian wrestling with the visual satisfaction derived by the artist from the contemplation of the same ensemble:

A winding stair in one of the round towers leads to the oldest portion of the Palace, commonly known as 'Queen Mary's apartments'. Although the guides who professionally show these rooms annually to an endless succession of visitors probably tell as many fables as the rest of their craft, it is impossible to follow them through the scene of so many strange incidents without a feeling of lively interest, even while it is neces-

sary to preserve a wholesome scepticism regarding the fingers that have accomplished certain needle work, the people who have slept in certain beds, and especially the genuineness of some paintings. The old panelling, the mouldering bedsteads and high backed chairs, and even the miserable pictures making visible progress towards decay, convey a more real effect of venerable age to the mind than many antiquities whose far better claims to genuineness are neutralised by their more spruce and well kept condition.

Burton brought the same critical eye to the celebrated bloodstains:

It is not crusted like recently deposited blood, but has an unctuous appearance, is evidently impregnated with the structure of the wood, and seems to justify its reputed quality of being ineradicable'.

20: COUNT ARTUR POTOKI'S
RENTED DRAWING ROOM IN MORAY PLACE, EDINBURGH
1840

Surprisingly this watercolour, made as a souvenir of a visit to Edinburgh by a Polish nobleman, is the only contemporary view of the interior of a later New Town house. The glimpse of a Palace front through the window reveals that this rented house was in Moray Place. It is perhaps no accident that this square is the best documented in Edinburgh because the magnificent scale of the houses rivalled any in London and it set a new standard with many earlier houses being altered to bring them into line. The building papers for No. 3 survive including furnishing estimates from William Trotter whose furniture making business had boomed with the expansion of the New Town. It is a measure of the degree to which these houses were in thrall to social conventions that the rare survival of the dining room furniture at No. 31 matches the description of the estimate for No. 3 of c.1825. Although this view is dated 1840, the drawing room had clearly been fitted up earlier and, again, the furniture reflects the estimate for No. 3.

The principal floor of the house was devoted to the Drawing Rooms and the large double doors could be folded back to accommodate the large parties or 'routs' held by each hostess at least once a season. Because they functioned as a unified suite, the front and back drawing rooms were decorated and furnished identically. As a result of their wedge-shaped plan, some houses in Moray Place had up to three drawing rooms in addition to an ante-room, forming a circuit round the stairwell. Nothing but the best was deemed suitable for drawing rooms which were regarded as state rooms. The chimneypiece is of the most expensive pure white statuary marble in severe Grecian style. Gilding played a prominent part in Drawing Rooms and it is more than likely that the walls are stencilled in gold on a textured ground following one of the patent recipes of D. R. Hay, the city's leading house-painter. The curtains in No. 3 were of silk with a pleated valence and hung from 'A rich brass Cornice' and the curtains were draped over 'brass curtain bands'. The floor was covered with 'a Brussels carpet of best quality, a fine Wilton hearth Rug' and there was 'a floor cover of mixture drugget' as shown here. Mahogany was no longer deemed elegant enough for the best drawing rooms and all the drawing room furniture in No. 3 was of 'Patent polished real rosewood'. There was a variety of tables including a 'Loo', 'a pair of handsome pillar and claw Card tables to suit', 'a Sofa Table', 'A Handsome Ladies Work table of fine Elm' and 'two handsome square real rosewood Tea Poys on therm'd pillars and plinths'. There was a similarly varied collection of seat furniture also of rosewood and covered in silk with 'Overall Slips of printed cotton'. At No. 3 there was a 'whole back' sofa and a 'Grecian Ottoman with one high end' but here there seems to be a matching pair of couches. Two stuffed arm chairs and twelve 'very fine' chairs completed the set. The 'fine chimney mirror in a gilded frame ' at No. 3 may also have been in the Louis style like this one and Trotter particularly liked this style for drawing rooms because it gave the opportunity for a lavish display of gilding. This eclectic mixing of styles was condemned by the Scottish design reformers William Dyce and C. H. Wilson in their *Letter to Lord Meadowbank*, 1837.

The viewpoint of the artist excludes the finest piece in these Drawing Rooms because to balance the chimneypiece in No. 3 Trotter supplied 'a Splendid Commode of Fancy wood with truss legs highly ornamented with marble top and mirror under' above which was 'a Very fine Mirror for over ditto in a handsome gilded frame'.

Facing: 20

21: SIR JOHN ROBISON AT 13 RANDOLPH CRESCENT, EDINBURGH
1840

It is ironic, perhaps, that the most perfunctory illustrations in this book should also record Scotland's most original contribution to interior design. Medium and message, however, were in close harmony because these crude woodcuts were geared to the mass dissemination of information through the rise of the illustrated magazine. The doyen of editors was John Claudius Loudon, among whose many titles, some of which were produced simultaneously, was *An Encyclopaedia of Cottage, Farm and Villa Architecture and Furniture*, (1839). Loudon's task was eased by a body of enthusiastic correspondents whose number included Sir John Robison, a fellow Scot and a brilliant inventor. The son of an outstanding professor of natural philosophy at Edinburgh University, the range of Robison's interests was typical of the 'Mod-

ern Athens' and he had the means as well as the talent to develop his ideas to the full. It was perhaps no surprise that he should have been attracted by the decorative experiments of David Ramsay Hay, the city's leading house painter who sought to establish his profession on scientific principles rather than the caprices of personal taste. Hay harnessed colour theory to his business and went on to elucidate pure aesthetics. These interests could never have found practical expression without the enthusiastic support of such scientifically inclined intellectuals as Sir John who were prepared to offer up their own drawing rooms for experiment. Robison made his first appearance in Loudon's pages through the publication of a description of his drawing room which had been decorated by Hay. This had a scientific colour scheme in

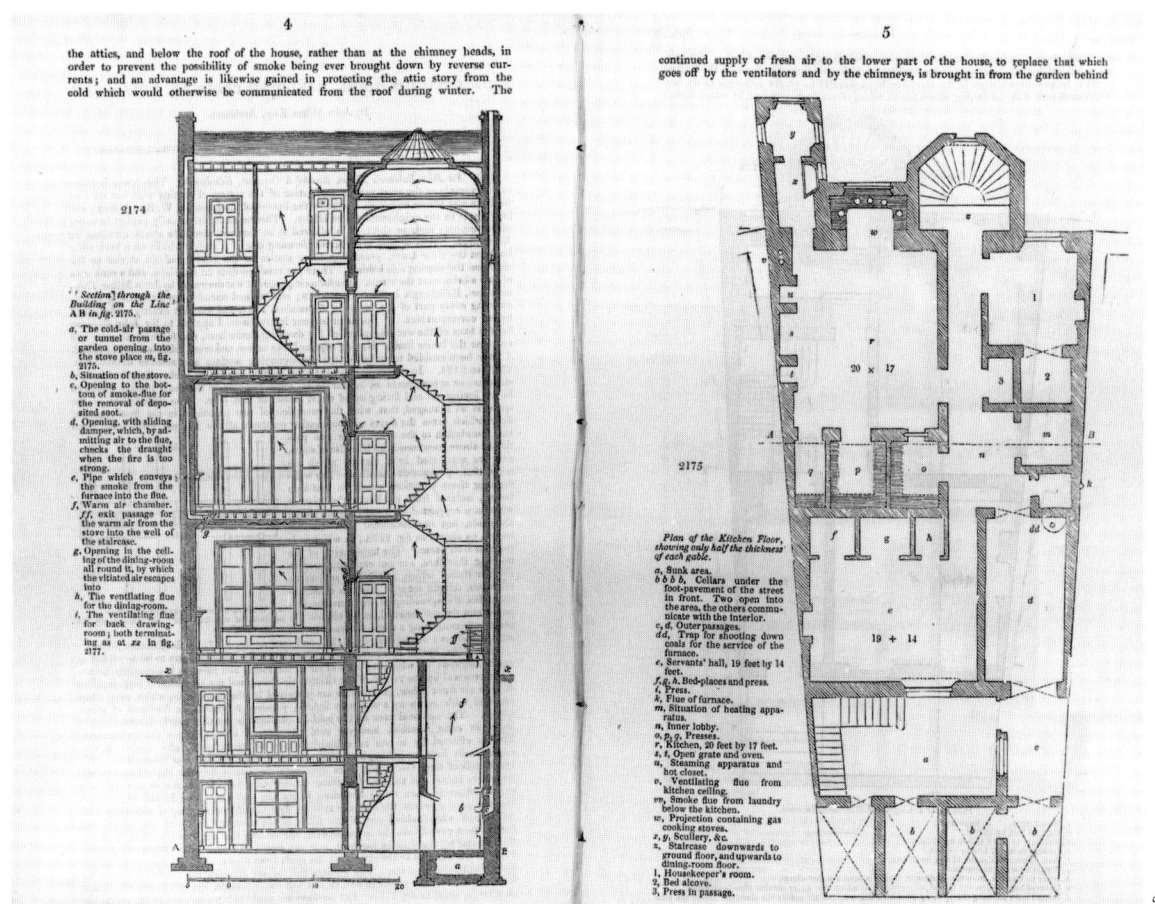

which 'pure' crimson was deliberately contrasted with green in conjunction with white ceiling and woodwork. The crimson painted walls were textured to imitate morocco leather (which was apparently so realistic that they had deceived a bookbinder 'who wondered where such enormous skins were to be obtained'). The walls were over-stencilled with gilt rosettes. Other aspects of the room were subject to the same rational scrutiny that typified Edinburgh during this period: 'The window hangings are of the simplest form: mere large curtains, without draperies or fringes. They hang in vertical lines, and catch no dust.' Sir John designed their supports himself in the form of gilded wooden rods whose surface was protected from scratches by brass fillets let into their upper surface bearing the rings [21c]. The curtains

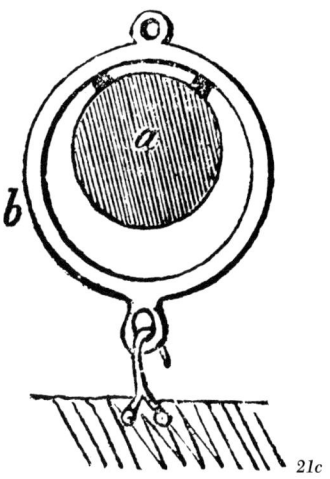

21c

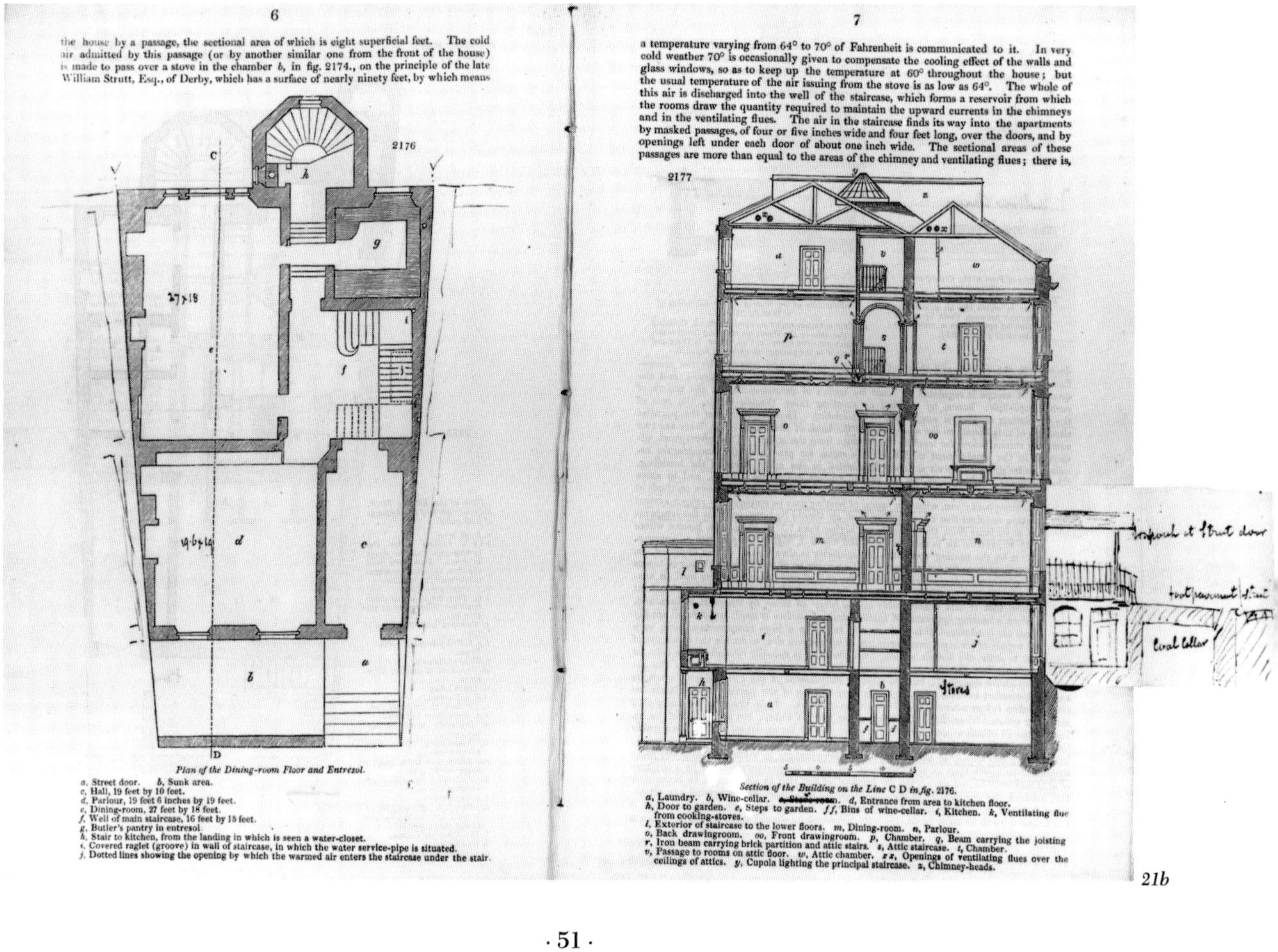

6

the house by a passage, the sectional area of which is eight superficial feet. The cold air admitted by this passage (or by another similar one from the front of the house) is made to pass over a stove in the chamber b, in fig. 2174., on the principle of the late William Strutt, Esq., of Derby, which has a surface of nearly ninety feet, by which means

2176

27×18

14·6×14

Plan of the Dining-room Floor and Entresol.

a. Street door.   b. Sunk area.
c. Hall, 19 feet by 10 feet.
d. Parlour, 19 feet 6 inches by 19 feet.
e. Dining-room, 27 feet by 18 feet.
f. Well of main staircase, 16 feet by 15 feet.
g. Butler's pantry in entresol.
h. Stair to kitchen, from the landing in which is seen a water-closet.
i. Covered raglet (groove) in wall of staircase, in which the water service-pipe is situated.
j. Dotted lines showing the opening by which the warmed air enters the staircase under the stair.

7

a temperature varying from 64° to 70° of Fahrenheit is communicated to it.   In very cold weather 70° is occasionally given to compensate the cooling effect of the walls and glass windows, so as to keep up the temperature at 60° throughout the house; but the usual temperature of the air issuing from the stove is as low as 64°.   The whole of this air is discharged into the well of the staircase, which forms a reservoir from which the rooms draw the quantity required to maintain the upward currents in the chimneys and in the ventilating flues.   The air in the staircase finds its way into the apartments by masked passages, of four or five inches wide and four feet long, over the doors, and by openings left under each door of about one inch wide.   The sectional areas of these passages are more than equal to the areas of the chimney and ventilating flues; there is,

2177

Section of the Building on the Line C D in fig. 2176.

a, Laundry.   b, Wine-cellar.   d, Entrance from area to kitchen floor.
h, Door to garden.   e, Steps to garden.   f f, Bins of wine-cellar.   i, Kitchen.   k, Ventilating flue from cooking-stoves.
l, Exterior of staircase to the lower floors.   m, Dining-room.   n, Parlour.
o, Back drawingroom.   oo, Front drawingroom.   p, Chamber.   q, Beam carrying the joisting
r, Iron beam carrying brick partition and attic stairs.   s, Attic staircase.   t, Chamber.
v, Passage to rooms on attic floor.   w, Attic chamber.   xx, Openings of ventilating flues over the ceilings of attics.   y, Cupola lighting the principal staircase.   z, Chimney-heads.

21b

were operated by means of cords 'made very conspicuous' and which 'contribute to the general effect'. This had been suggested, however, 'by an old picture' rather than the application of pure reason. Although equally novel, it is difficult to see the practical justification for Sir John's idea of framing the overmantel glass with a frame composed of the same marble as the chimneypiece itself [21d]. Many of these features were also adopted by Hay for the drawing room of his own villa in Jordan Lane.

Sir John's inventive streak found fullest expression when he constructed his own house at 13 Randolph Crescent. This was the subject of a long adulatory description by John Milne published in 1840 as a supplement to Loudon's *Encyclopaedia*. Sir John's enthusiasm for gas lighting and more unusually, cooking apparatus, was appropriately partnered by his experiments with ventilation. The hot air heating system helped to draw in and distribute volumes of fresh air to replace that which had been vitiated by the gas. The house boasted steel beams supporting its partitions preventing vibration, a new method of dispersing snow from its gutters, improved ball-cocks, highly original door locks and Sir John even designed its furniture. The marble chimney-

glasses were repeated and Sir John seems to have had a matching marble console table and glass to balance the drawing room chimney – as did D. R. Hay at Jordan Lane. The decorations at Randolph Crescent were also by Hay. Although Sir John's study and the Dining Room were painted 'in imitation of wainscot', white was chosen for the staircase, the drawing rooms and their ante room. The morocco effect was repeated as was the gold-stencilling, which were high varnished, but Hay overlaid these with a further stencilled pattern in matt white which, according to Milne, gave 'the appearance of a lace dress over satin and spangles'. In spite of Hay's faith in the scientific basis of his schemes it must have been a disappointment that Sir John chose white ceilings on account of his personal taste. Only a few of his patrons could 'go the length of the most intense colours, or polychrome.' Hay stated in his attached explanation that 'with this last class I myself agree' but warned that 'if this be not done with the strictest attention to the laws of harmonious colouring the effect must be bad'. Sir John's house survives, but little is now apparent of the ingenuity which had once made it the Northern Athenian house *par excellence*.

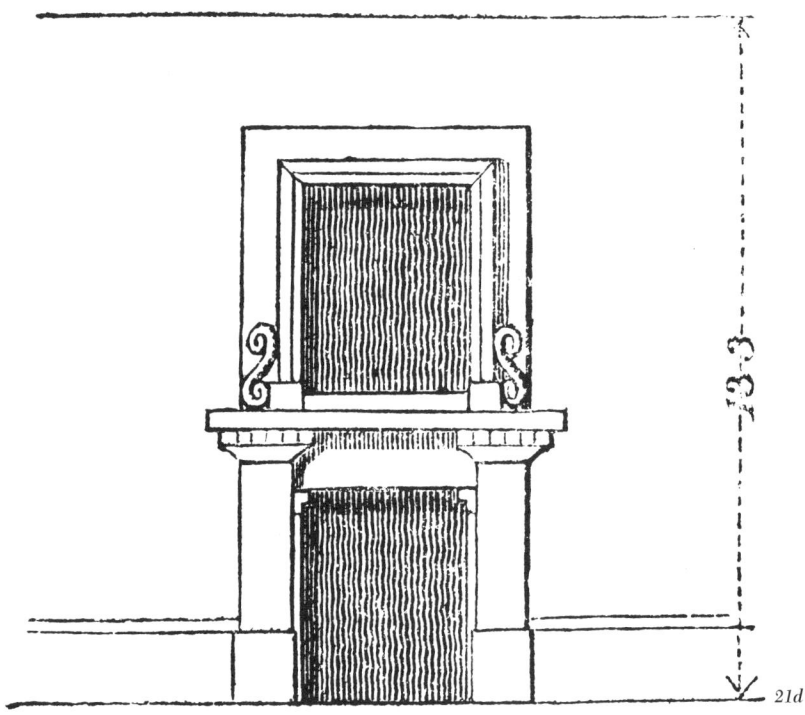

21d

22: QUEEN VICTORIA IS ENTERTAINED AT TAYMOUTH CASTLE
1842

The popular appeal of the young Queen Victoria's first visit to Scotland was reflected in the publication of two rival illustrated records of her progress from Edinburgh through the Perthshire highlands. Her sojourn at Taymouth, as guest of the Marquess of Breadalbane, was seen as the climax of the tour. The Castle was well-fitted to fulfil its role in the Highland spectacular, brilliantly directed by the Marquess, because it had been the object of lavish expenditure from the beginning of the nineteenth century. Until then, successive Earls of Breadalbane had been at pains to classicise their ancient stronghold and one writer had commented favourably that it 'looks well in its new coat and sash windows'. Under the influence of Picturesque taste, however, the modernised castle was deemed unworthy of its romantic setting amid the mountains at the head of Loch Tay and the first Marquess had employed the Elliots and Atkinson to Gothicise it. The results reflected the family's

great wealth deriving from almost 400,000 acres stretching from Perthshire to Argyll, but a certain indecisiveness on the part of the patron meant that there was much to be completed when the second Marquess succeeded in 1834. Gillespie Graham, the leading exponent of the Gothic in Scotland, was called in to this end and his main achievement was to rebuild the surviving western eighteenth-century pavilion in such a way that it deliberately broke the symmetry of the Elliots' design. Its interior contained a splendid suite of rooms which may have been intended as the Marquess's private apartment and this work must have been well-nigh finished when the Marquess received his intimation of the Queen's visit.

Gillespie Graham's mastery of the Gothic style owed a certain amount to team-work in that the archaeological intricacy of its detailing was due to A. W. N. Pugin who had a long and close relationship with him as the

22a

Overleaf: 22b

researchers James Macaulay and Lady Alexandra Wedgwood have recently uncovered. The success of their interiors also derived from the incorporation of actual antique fragments, and much early stained glass and carved oak was reset at Taymouth. For the execution of his architectural woodwork and tracery, Graham employed Trotter of Edinburgh and under his patronage the firm was transformed from the mass furnishers of Edinburgh's New Town into Gothic specialists. In 1842 the Marquess also employed Frederick Crace and Son of London, but it is still not clear if they were merely applying the finishing touches to rooms that were substantially complete, or whether their employment reflected a last minute panic lest the rooms could not be considered fit for the sovereign. The result was an extravaganza on a generalised Troubadour theme rather than one intrinsically Scottish, and the Marquess's Highland dress of plaid patterned velvet was symptomatic of the stage-properties. The only local elements deployed for the occasion were the pearls in the silver-gilt handmirror on the Queen's toilette table which came from the Tay.

Graham's principal addition was the Banner Hall which linked the Elliots' main block to the refitted West Pavilion. The lithograph from *Queen Victoria in Scotland* shows it arranged for the Grand Ball held on the Friday evening of the Queen's visit and at the moment when four gentlemen – as distinct from the rough Highlanders who performed *outside* the Castle – danced the 'Reel of Tulloch' at her special request before her dias at the south end of the Hall. To create an authentic effect, Graham's great canopied chimney-piece was of unpainted stone rather than marble and Trotter's intricately carved panelling, and pair of interior porches, were left in natural oak. Above the walls painted as plain 'stone', the great roof trusses were grained in a matching imitation of oak, and framed ceiling panels were emblazoned with the heraldry of the Campbells of Breadalbane explaining their descent from the Scottish royal line. Crace charged £350 for this decorative painting which included the necessary research. The firm also supplied the banners which gave the room its name for £3.15s each and it was characteristic of the bogus and

entirely decorative effect that the suits of demi-armour beneath them, far from being venerable Campbell relics, also hailed from the same wareroom in Wigmore Street at £7 each, although some of the 'weapons' were made up on site. The great traceried window was filled both with 'old German glass' and a modern imitation eking it out to fit. On the evening of the ball it was illuminated from without.

The right hand of the two interior porches led through the Library Gallery into the Library proper and the steel-engraving from Sir Thomas Dick Lauder's *The Royal Progress in Scotland* employs a degree of artistic licence in omitting the glazed doors of the Library, but faithfully records the dramatic effect of Crace's upholstery which comprised the most expensive component in their accounts: 'To making up a suite of rich Portière Curtains for Entrance to Library the whole bordered with Crimson Velvet and trimmed with rich fringes gimp &c and with handsome tassel curtain holders… £30.' The Library was inspired by 'Crosby Hall in London' and Trotter's estimate of June 1839 explains that the shutters were made up to frame old carvings. The vigour of the old work may have been responsible for infecting the new with a medieval richness of detail and no two of the pillars separating the glazed cases are alike. In his description, Lauder, who was a leading exponent of the Picturesque in Scotland and a connoisseur of art manufactures by profession, employed a torrent of superlatives. He considered the Library to be the 'gem' of the Castle and compared it to the Alhambra. During the Queen's visit the West Wing was made over as her private suite creating 'a little private palace of her own', with the Library forming her sitting room. Although she is shown resting on a sofa of modern form it is clear that the majority of the furnishings, like the curtains made up from 'old velvet', were antique and some of the chairs look early Georgian in character. Amid this richness there was little even for Crace to do beyond painting descriptive plaques of the contents over the bookcases. The ancient character was probably intended to be furthered by the carpet imitating an 'oak' parquet which harmonised with the genuine parquet of the Banner Hall.

23: THE REVEREND JOHN SIME COMMISSIONS
A MEMORIAL OF TRINITY COLLEGE HOSPITAL, EDINBURGH
1845

Trinity College and its Hospital was probably founded by Mary of Gueldres, the Queen of James II. As a result of this royal solicitude, the church was one of Scotland's finest examples of Gothic architecture, while the soundness of the Hospital's charitable purpose ensured that it even came through the Reformation unscathed. Under new direction by the Town Council, the Hospital was adapted to receive and care for poor old people. Sadly, the founder could not have foreseen that the chosen site was to be pinpointed in 1843 as lying directly in the path of the ideal route for the East Coast Railway which was to connect Edinburgh with London. The announcement that the Chapel and Hospital buildings had been sold to the Railway Directors caused a 'sensation' and marked the beginning of the greatest preservation scandal in nineteenth-century Scotland. As a compromise it was decided that the Church would be carefully dismantled and reconstructed on another site, but the Hospital,

which was devoid of Gothic elegancies, was soon 'levelled with the dust'.

It must have been a devastating blow for the patients whose lives seem to have been so agreeable that when one of their number, Miss Violet Maitland, came into an unexpected legacy in 1842, she paid back every penny of the charitable sums that had been expended on her upkeep and asked to be allowed to end her days within its walls. The Chaplain's distress at the loss of his home must have been compounded by his antiquarian enthusiasms. With great presence of mind, however, he commissioned the artist, William Douglas, to make a series of views, while Sime himself, who had had some training as an architect before turning to the church, drew up a measured survey.

The general form of the Chaplain's Room as shown in Douglas's view, probably reflects the 1728 refitting of the Hospital. The double-doors concealed a press-bed.

23a

The furnishings and their arrangement reflects Sime's antiquarian tastes and everything within it was at least half-a-century old in 1845. The only concession to modernity is the gas bracket in its customary place on the mantleshelf which had probably been added to the marble chimneypiece at the same time. Although a card table has been set up near the window for reading, the Chippendale chairs are stiffly ranged round the walls in eighteenth-century fashion and the pictures have been composed in a formal pattern on the chimney-wall. The draw-up curtains and the Neo-Classical coffering of the flatwoven Scotch carpet must date from the 1780s.

That this old-fashioned look was deliberately cultivated is confirmed by the companion view of the Matron's Room which shows that by contrast, she has succumbed to every fashionable whim. Although her seat furniture is even more antediluvian than the Chaplain's, the other plates in this book show that seventeenth-century chairs were enjoying a fashionable revival. The Matron has a new Grecian-style chimneypiece and a modern grate which contrasts with the Chaplain's old stove-grate. Her room is cheerfully wallpapered and both her carpet with its matching hearthrug and the form of her curtains with a pleated pelmet are modern and cosy, like her elegant counterweighted gas fitting. In his *Memorials*, Lord Cockburn paints a vivid description of a visit to the Hospital and its cheery inmates which makes its loss the more poignantly tragic. He reveals that the Matron's parrot was a 'Blue' while the 'brass wire cage, with doors and windows like a Cathedral' in the window held a canary. Sadly, propriety prevented Douglas from completing his record with a view of her bedroom which caused Lord Cockburn to exclaim, 'What a coverlet of patchwork!'.

23b

The Baronial and Ecclesiastical Antiquities of Scotland is the most beautiful book ever devoted to this subject and includes a number of interior views. Although it followed in a tradition of topographical publication, it had a new specifically architectural purpose as a source book and it was soon established as the bible of the Baronial revival. Its origins lay in a collaboration between William Burn, Scotland's leading country house architect, and Robert Billings, a specialist English architectural illustrator, who had learned his outstanding skills during his apprenticeship to John Britton. The handsome result also owed much to Blackwood the publisher, who selected John Hill Burton, a frequent contributor to *Blackwood's Magazine*, to prepare the historical descriptions for the letter-press. The link during this period between antiquarian draughtsmanship and modern designs in historic styles was well illustrated by

Billings' earlier collaboration with Sir Jeffrey Wyattville in the rebuilding of Windsor Castle. In his choice of views for this sumptuous survey, Billings was particularly drawn to decorative plasterwork which was especially relevant for architects like Burn who were seeking to compose Picturesque interiors to match their elaborately detailed exteriors in a Scottish idiom. Although Billings laid great stress on the accuracy of his studies as against the more slovenly methods of his predecessors like Francis Grose, it is clear that he brought a highly selective eye to this aspect of his activities. Few interiors had been as untouched by time as he might have wished and one can sense his disappointment at the recent sprucing up of Glamis [24a] in Burton's accompanying description:

> *In the great hall – the beautiful pargeted roof which is depicted in the accompanying plate – there are several*

24a

pictures – some of them of no small value. They have lately been restored, and their frames have been gilt, so that their glossy exhibition-room-like freshness is in contrast with the grim antiquity of the surrounding objects. Some specimens of old armour – chiefly oriental, and not of much interest or value – are shown to visitors. More worthy of observation is a clothes chest containing some court dresses of the seventeenth century, still glittering in not entirely obliterated finery, among which is preserved the motley raiment of the family fool.

It must have been tiresome to be constantly directed by ignorant guides to notice unimportant trivia, and it is a reminder of how many historic rooms at this time, to an informed eye, must have been full of incongruous and anachronistic flotsam. Such experiences must have contributed to the educational zeal that fired Billings' endeavours, and which he saw as fundamental for the preservation of Scotland's historic buildings. Many were

still regarded as mere quarries of material. He included an especial tribute in his introduction to the 'ministers of the Presbyterian Church' who were the only fount of knowledge during his 'lonely wanderings from beaten tracks'. Perhaps rather surprisingly, Billings was accompanied on one of his Scottish forays by his wife as a letter of 1845 describes:

We intend to be wanderers just getting lodgings for the time we may be in a particular locality – my wife is studying drawing confoundedly hard so as to be useful as well as ornamental.

During these travels they assiduously sought fresh subscribers in a process which Billings described in angling terms. In his published perspectives his solution was to omit later accretions as far as possible and thus at Winton [24b], although he included the Neo-Classical bas reliefs, introduced to reduce the original width of the fireplace, he replaced the gilt 'Louis' furniture with a suite of fantasy chairs of his own. The chair shown in the

24b

adjoining King Charles' Room [24c] must surely also be invention. However, the eighteenth-century circular topped tripod table in the Drawing Room really existed and is shown frozen in the same position in a later photograph [24d]. It is clear that the furniture is arranged for purely pictorial effect and balance. The absence of recent furnishings gives his figures in modern dress a surreal quality. The unreality is heightened through his having deliberately eschewed dramatic effects of light and shade in favour of clarity of detail as his introduction explains. The surviving preparatory drawings for the plates of Craigievar [24e,f] have a surprising freshness for eyes accustomed to the sombre finished engravings. A comparison between the two bears out his claim that his copyists, who were drawn from the finest engravers like John le Keux, faithfully followed his drawings. Billings' years of experience in book production developed his flair for telling composition and this is particularly noticeable in his far from obvious view of Mary Queen of Scots' Bedchamber at

24d

24c

Holyrood [24g] in which he highlighted the way the southern window frames the crowned cupola over the main entrance. In spite of his diligence, Billings' book was faulted for its old-fashioned, purely pictorial approach, by critics like James Fergusson, who regretted the absence of plans and analysis. Billings subsequently practised as an architect in his own right and his mastery of geometry and perspective found a further outlet in his writings on the design of Gothic tracery.

24e

24

24f

25: JOSEPH NEIL PATON'S ANTIQUARIAN *COTTAGE ORNEE* AT WOOERS-ALLEY DUNFERMLINE BY WALLER HUGH PATON
1848

Although at first sight this interior with its pensive costume figure seems entirely fanciful, it is probably a faithful record by the young artist, Waller Hugh Paton, of his family's unusual home. In 1848 he exhibited 'The Antique Room at Wooers-Alley by Firelight' and this large watercolour, which remained in the possession of the artist's descendants, fits that title. Wooers-Alley had been built by his father, Joseph Neil Paton, who was a native of Dunfermline. After receiving the necessary training at the Board of Manufactures' Drawing Academy at Edinburgh, Paton returned home as a designer for the important local damask-weaving industry and also to teach design in the Academy's branch school there. Paton was an enthusiastic antiquarian and he must have been fired by the ancient glory of the town which had once been the capital of Scotland. Its illustrious past was commemorated in the Abbey with Bruce's tomb and the ruins of the Royal Palace. Although the name of his house conjures up an urban setting, a surviving sketch shows that it was really a villa, or rather, through its fanciful Gothic character, a *cottage ornée*. Dunfermline seems to have supplied plentiful quantities of old oak and many of its treasures seem to have been donated as the house took on something of a public character as one of the town's star attractions. It is perhaps little wonder, that, conditioned by this remarkable environment where studio props blended into domestic life, all of Paton's three children were to become artists. The eldest son, Sir Noel Paton, was the most celebrated through his fairy pictures and his patronage by Queen Victoria. In his own house at 33 George Square, Edinburgh, he replicated the character of Wooers-Alley and it too was as much a museum as a private house.

Queen Victoria's acquisition of a Highland estate in 1848 was one of the most unexpected events of nineteenth-century Scotland which was to have far reaching repercussions in many areas of Scottish life. No Scottish house has been more frequently recorded than Balmoral and this reflects the mutual regard in which it was held by both the Queen and her subjects. Because the Queen acquired the lease without having visited the spot there was an immediate need for illustrations. When she was able to purchase Balmoral in 1852 the opportunity was taken to resite the castle to take greater advantage of the views along the Dee Valley. A local Aberdeen photographer, George Washington Wilson, was employed during the rebuilding to take progress photographs which were despatched to Prince Albert in London. The spot selected for the new castle necessitated the demolition of the old house but the Queen took care to make a record of its internal appearance [26a–d]. She commissioned the artist James Giles, who

had particular experience of recording the castles of Aberdeenshire through a long standing commission from Lord Aberdeen. The Queen may also have known of his view of the Drawing Room at Haddo [18]. Giles' resulting watercolours have not only an intrinsic interest as records of the Queen's first Scottish years, but they are also the most beautiful and meticulously detailed views of any Scottish house.

Old Balmoral Castle had been virtually rebuilt by Sir Robert Gordon who had acquired the lease in 1830 from the Earl of Fife, and employed the architect, John Smith of Aberdeen, to modernise it. When the Queen took on the lease after his death in 1847 the house came complete with its furnishings. Although the internal arrangement was adapted for royal usage, and the Queen and the Prince added their personal possessions, there is reason to think that the general appearance of the rooms reflects Sir Robert's choices rather than the Queen's. His taste seems to have been conventional and the

26a

rooms are very plain with unornamented cornices and slab-like Grecian chimneypieces, enlivened by graining and colourful carpets and wallpapers. The name 'Balmoral' occurs in the volumes of designs by the Edinburgh furniture-makers, Trotter, and so this firm may have been employed by Sir Robert. They probably supplied the carved oak chimneypiece which was almost the only item to be transferred to the new Balmoral. The dining chairs, however, are far from being the most expensive type. The room is identical to hundreds of other Scottish dining rooms with its black marble chimneypiece, plain painted walls, oak graining and the Turkey rug was the norm. The Billiard Room with its simple bookcases is just as severe. The Queen seems to have appropriated Sir Robert's Drawing Room for her bedroom because it has the standard white statuary marble chimneypiece, and both the doorcases and the grate are more elaborate than those of the other rooms. The stags' heads in her sitting room were the staple of

Deeside decoration and are a reminder of the principal source of Deeside's attractions for sportsmen for at least a generation previous to the Queen's arrival. A deerskin rug has been placed under the writing table. The principal rooms all have fitted carpets of a superior kind and none of them appear to be flatwoven Scotch. The Queen's pleasure in Giles' splendid watercolours, the product of so much labour, was marred as Lady Delia Millar has described in *Queen Victoria's Life in the Scottish Highlands* by the fact that their format was too large to allow them to be mounted in her existing Balmoral albums and Giles was humiliatingly asked to colour a set of photographic reductions for this purpose. This experience must have been enough to make him give up recording interiors.

The new house was no less assiduously depicted and two of its interiors became known to a wide public through the coloured lithographs which the Queen herself published in her *Leaves from the Journal of our Life*

26b

in *The Highlands* of 1864 which was part of her memorial to Prince Albert whose death in 1861 left her devastated. The Queen chose to show both her own and the Prince's Sitting Rooms [26e,f]. Interestingly, although they are very much more thoroughly worked out as a result of the Prince's exacting approach, their essential character is little different from old Balmoral. In building for themselves without interference from government departments, the Royal family successfully continued the spirit of their first holiday home although there is a new stress on Scottishness in the tartan carpets and thistle chintz which unify the two suites. The English firm of Holland & Company was employed to finish to rooms. Stags heads have been eliminated from the private apartments and were confined to the circulation areas. The Prince also preserved the informal character by electing to decorate the house with engravings rather than paintings.

26e

2

26c

This simplicity and practicality is far removed from the Ballroom [26g] which had a theatrical character reminiscent of Taymouth [22b], which had first drawn the Queen to the Highlands. The absurdities of its decorations which diversified the stags heads at intervals with a ludicrous suspended stuffed eagle and what appear to be sporrans strung up like sporting trophies, arose from the responsibility for its appearance having been delegated to James Grieve, a theatre designer. It is a reminder of the rather bogus side of Balmoral and the Queen's attempt to stage-manage the survival of traditional patterns of Highland life to the extent of compulsory kilt wearing. The Queen's enthusiastic patronage of George Washington Wilson led to his being granted permission to sell his photographs of Balmoral and they thus frequently appear in albums of the period and survived into the age of the postcard.

26g

26d

Following the lead of the professional artists, amateurs too began to make records of the interiors of their homes. Curiously, there do not seem to be nearly so many drawings of Scottish rooms as their English counterparts and the former tend to be dated to the mid-century while the latter begin rather earlier. This set of views is of particular interest because both the house and its furnishings are well documented in the family papers. East Warriston is a substantial Edinburgh villa begun in 1808 by Andrew Bonar, an Edinburgh banker and partner in Ramsay and Bonar. It was probably designed by the architect and builder, Robert Burn, and initially, like many villas in the vicinity of Edinburgh, was primarily a summer residence because the family also had a town house. From the early 1830s it was occupied throughout the year by his son, William, who was also a banker and his newly-married wife, Lilly.

Bonar kept meticulous account books, as befitted his profession, and the purchase of many of the items depicted by his daughter, Miss Margaret Bonar c.1850 can be traced.

Remarkably the house survived intact into this century, so the views can also be related to his great-grand-daughter's memories. Miss Bonar's watercolours seem to have been made prior to the family's departure to spend several years in the south but the accounts show that furnishings had been added throughout the late 1840s. The Dining Room [27a] has the recessed plaster panels that were to be fashionable in New Town dining rooms. The wide Venetian window frames a spectacular panorama of the Calton Hill and Edinburgh lying to the south of East Warriston. The woodwork appears to be oak-grained but the wall-face has been painted as stone colour, with the ceiling tinted to tone in. The window

27

curtains were supplied by Allardyce in 1833 and their double draperies cope with the complexity of the Venetian window. All the carpets were bought from Richard Whytock. In July 1838 the Drawing Room carpet was described as having 'a brown ground, rich gold coloured leafy pattern and bright bouquets of flowers'. The open back Grecian dining chairs are like those made by Trotter for Moray Place c.1825. The three dinner tables must have been very flexible for different sizes of party. Fitted carpets were unusual in dining rooms where a Turkey rug was the norm. The big horse-hair covered sofa, in addition to the two arm chairs may also suggest that the room functioned as the family's everyday sitting room. The painting on the right by Crawford shows Craigends House and was purchased in 1845 for £30 with 5 guineas for the gilt frame. Bonar had also collected landscapes by Hugh 'Grecian' Williams,

Nasmyth and Andrew Wilson. Bonar's great-grand-daughter Mrs Ashford, remembers family prayers being held in this room with extra benches brought in for the maids and placed in front of the sideboard which faced the windows. The view of the Library [27c] shows fitted bookcases and similar curtains. The arch-headed section of the cases on the right concealed a jib door. The gilt 'Louis' pier glass was purchased for £15 at the sale of Kimmerghame, a family house, in 1847. The Library was connected to the adjoining Drawing Room by folding doors and their chimney-piece, curtains and fitted carpets were *en suite*. The chair in front of the fire with its upheld arms was christened 'little come'. The Drawing Room [27b] appears to have gilt wallpaper. The 'Louis' chimney-glass had integral candle-branches as described in the 1924 Inventory and may be that purchased from S. Cooper in London for £40 during 1841. The seat

27b

furniture was supplied by Morison in 1847 and included 'an Elmwood sofa £12.15, pillows and velvet cover £1.15, 4 Rosewood Drawing Room chairs and slips £9.16, and a Prie Dieu Chair £4'. In 1844 the same firm had made a 'Loo table' which may be that covered with the red cloth. P. Robertson charged £7.17 in 1845 for the 'Marchioness sofa' but it also appears as a 'Duchess sofa' and is probably the double-backed one on the left. The same furniture maker altered the 'old oak cabinet' after it had been purchased in London in 1843 for £9.10. It gave a fashionable antiquarian touch to this Neo-Classical room.

The Drawing Room also contained a number of wedding presents including the 'Grand Rosewood Pianoforte from my brother John' valued at £150 and the 'Handsome Drawing Room Clock with Glass shade and compensation pendulum (English made) from James'. The letter from his brother James which accompanied this gift survives and describes its purchase 'from Hawley' and its design as being 'the first he has ever made of the style'. The case was ormolu and it has been given place of honour on the chimneypiece. East Warriston was comfortable rather than expensively elegant, and taken together, the drawings and accounts show the furnishings were augmented from time to time by new pieces reflecting changing fashions and needs.

2

28: SARAH SHERWOOD CLARKE STAYS AT ARDCHEANOCHROCHAN INN DURING HER TOUR OF THE TROSSACHS
1854

This exceptionally rare view of a Highland inn comes from an album of attractive watercolours recording a tour of Scotland by Sarah Sherwood Clarke, of whom nothing is known. Her route followed a stereotyped pattern and inevitably took in the Trossachs whose outstanding natural charms had been heightened by Sir Walter Scott's *Lady of the Lake*, making it a prime destination.

The inn had its beginnings as a mere cottage but this drawing shows that an improvised timber structure, with a large area of glass to the prospect, had been erected in an attempt to cope with the ever-increasing flocks of tourists. As a more permanent and doubtless profitable solution, the local landowner, Lord Willoughby de Eresby had commissioned his architect, George Kennedy, to design an hotel in 1852. Sarah shows a distant view of this with its distinctive steep conical turrets, but her sketch of the communal breakfast room in the temporary structure suggests that the amenities of the new building had yet to come into full commission. The roughness of the furnishings complementing the rustic dining room, is probably an accurate depiction because her album includes an accomplished view of Mary Queen of Scots' Bed Chamber at Holyrood.

29: DAVID ANDERSON OF MOREDUN'S
ROUND DRAWING ROOM AT 98 GEORGE STREET, EDINBURGH
1858

Although the Scots were enthusiastic pioneer photographers, there were obvious technical difficulties in recording interiors. It is quite exceptionally rare to have three views of a single room from so early a date. The occasion for the photographs was probably that 98 George Street had been sold for conversion to masonic halls and its days as a family home were over. Although the house dates from the end of the eighteenth century and would initially have had simple furniture like the Allans' at 28 Queen Street [9], the photographs show that, in common with so many other New Town houses, its rooms were refurnished in the 1820s to compete with the splendour of Moray Place. The view through to the front drawing room shows that characteristically both rooms are furnished *en suite* with matching fitted carpets so that they could function as a single unit to accommodate large parties and 'routs'. In keeping with late Georgian taste the columns have been painted to

resemble marble in both rooms, the door has been grained and high-varnished and the pier-glasses and curtain boxes are gilded to reflect the drawing rooms status as state rooms. The ottoman seat upholstered in chintz and following the curve of the walls seems to have been a common piece of Edinburgh drawing room furniture at this time and must have been invaluable for large gatherings. The round centre table is piled high with books, and posies of fresh flowers – perhaps from the Andersons' greenhouse at Moredun, their country villa near Edinburgh – surround an *objet de vertu* under its glass dome. An unconventional and individual note is struck only by the prominently displayed old master art collection which has outgrown the available wallspace and whose importance is reflected by their elaborate Louis gilded frames. The photographs are stereoscopic views which would have allowed the family to wallow in nostalgia and which show up the intricate detail of the furnishings.

29a

29b

29c

This watercolour is significant because it is one of the very few views of an interior to grace the Architectural Section of annual exhibitions of the Royal Scottish Academy during the Victorian period. No Scottish architect was more assiduous in sending in his work than David Bryce and from 1851 (when he was elected an Associate) until his death in 1876 the exhibition rooms featured huge watercolour perspectives of his latest designs. Because they represented executed work, they not only demonstrated his professional probity in giving satisfaction to a range of wealthy clients, but must have been instrumental in hooking future patrons who aspired to the same mode of life.

Bryce was to prove the master of the Baronial Revival and The Glen must have been one of his happiest commissions. Charles Tennant purchased the estate in 1852 and had at his command one of the largest industrial fortunes in Scotland deriving from his family's celebrated bleach and chemical works at St Rollox, near

Glasgow. A old house was pulled down to leave Bryce with an unusually free hand in his design for the new mansion which was begun in 1855. In both that year and in 1856 the exteriors were featured in the Royal Scottish Academy Exhibitions. The Billiard Room must, therefore, have been completed by 1860 when this watercolour was exhibited.

Although nominally fitted up as a Billiard Room, it was a far from typical domestic space. This first floor room was really a grand 'T'-shaped lobby, not only giving access to the suite of reception rooms (the open door leads into the drawing room) but also connecting the straight flight of steps from the ground floor entrance door to the principal stair. The glimpse of the main staircase framed through the double arch which greeted visitors at the top of the vestibule stair was a typically theatrical Bryce touch which he repeated in a number of his houses. It was thus the internal equivalent of the equally splendid external approach which led across a

bridge into a forecourt guarded by a stone archway. The design of ordinary domestic interiors like dining rooms and drawing rooms during the Victorian period rarely demanded any especial architectural skills and it is perhaps revealing of Bryce's artistic personality that he should have been able to seize this kind of opportunity to create such a very impressive effect.

As an attempt at a Baronial interior, the room obviously demonstrates the importance of Billings' researches but it is notable that the Mannerist detail follows English rather than Scots precedents. This is perhaps particularly surprising because Bryce, as a young man, seems to have made a particular study of old Scottish woodwork, according to Professor Alistair Rowan in his exhibition catalogue, *Mr David Bryce 1803–1876*. The mature Bryce, however, had a fondness for vigorous seventeenth-century style panelling with massive bolection projections. Bryce probably designed the bracketed console tables and the raised window seat, which would have been a good vantage point for watching a game of Billiards, but the other furnishings seem fanciful. Although his office may have set up the per-

spective, his flashy Royal Scottish Academy submissions must have been delegated to professional artists. Sadly, their names have not been recorded and the only signature that ever appeared on their ghosted efforts was Bryce's own. It was doubtless the artist who dreamed up the furniture and the rather vaguely patterned carpet but presumably it would have been on the architect's own instruction that the scene should become a study of prosperous domestic life and order.

It cannot have been bad for business that a Victorian papa should associate a Bryce house with contented children learning to master their powers of co-ordination under the supervision of their governess with an equally well behaved and sensible breed of dog alongside. The butler not only shows off the staircase but, like the decanter and glasses on the side-table, demonstrates that this is a hospitable household. The ancestral portraits (one of which has an historicist frame) the armour and the antlers are surely less to supply a fake ancestry for the Tennants than necessarily to continue the period flavour set by the fretwork ceiling and pannelling.

31a

31: HOLYROOD IS RENOVATED FOR QUEEN VICTORIA
1863

When Queen Victoria made her first visit to Scotland in 1842 the arrangements which prevailed for her uncle, George IV's state visit were simply repeated. The Queen also enjoyed the more modern comforts of Dalkeith Palace [31a]. It was intended to hold a similar drawing room at Holyrood and the Throne Room was rehung with 'crimson merino damask' but at the last minute a case of scarlet fever at the Palace placed it out of bounds for the Queen.

The decisive change in Holyrood's fortunes was a consequence of the Queen's acquisition of Balmoral. The derelict Palace was identified as a strategically placed overnight stop on the long train journey north. Since the necessary renovation, commanded by the Queen, arose to suit her personal convenience rather than from reasons of state, the treasury was reluctant to grant more than a minimal sum for what was ignomini-

ously classified as a 'temporary residence'. To the Scots, however, the Queen's return was hailed as an event of deep emotive significance and Robert Matheson, Principal Architect of the Office of works in Scotland, was determined that the character of the repairs should be worthy of the Palace's historical importance. His attitude probably hardened when his London masters doubted if there were any craftsmen in Scotland capable of doing work of Royal calibre.

Because there could be no hope of the wholesale eviction of the many grace-and-favour tenants, who included Scotland's premier peer, the Duke of Hamilton, and the Queen's own Lord Chamberlain, the only space available for the Queen was the old Royal Apartment on the first floor. Although this had been brought to the pitch of Carolean magnificence with some of the finest fretwork plaster ceilings in Britain, they lagged far

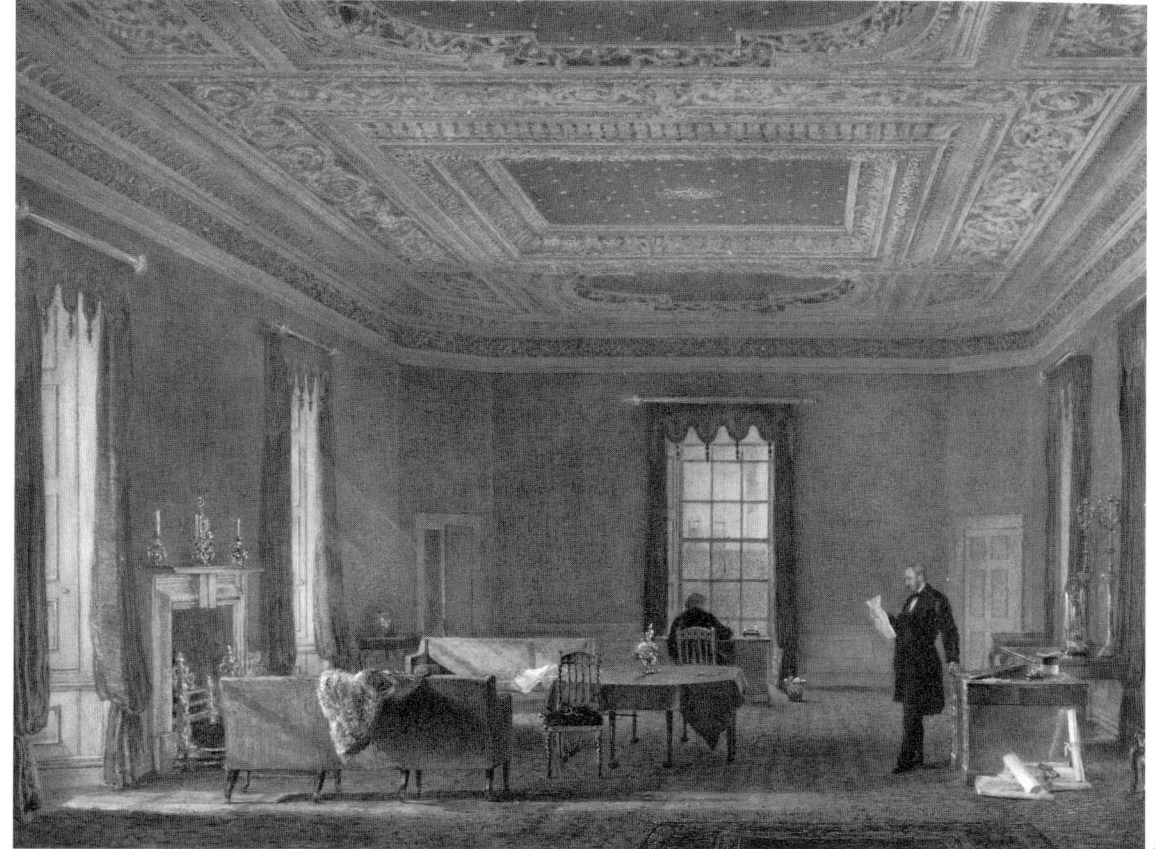

31b

behind the then current standards of comfort. To Victorian taste this drawback was somewhat offset by their antiquarian interest. The Lord Chamberlain had already instructed Trotter, the leading furniture maker in Edinburgh, to free the panelling of its disfiguring white paint but, with only £1500 to spend, there seemed little hope of recovering the original splendour. Matheson was undaunted and skilfully manoeuvred the contract for the redecoration into the hands of David Ramsay Hay, Edinburgh's leading house painter and pioneer interior decorator. As Matheson surely knew, Hay was unlikely to stint his ambitions for such an important national commission on account of a mere shortage of cash: the deficit would be met by Hay himself. Throughout his career Hay had adopted similar methods to encourage a more experimental climate of patronage. He almost always offered to paint over his more innovatory schemes 'free of all expense' if a client was dissatisfied and in 1846 he redecorated the Hall of the Society of

Arts 'in a superior style' for the cost of ordinary painting work. After the death of the Prince Consort in 1861, the Queen employed the artist, George M. Greig, to record her apartments at Holyrood as part of her memorial to their happy Highland holidays. Since none of Hay's scientifically contrived colour schemes have been preserved, Greig's watercolours are now the best record of what a Hay room was actually like. The Holyrood rooms are deficient in one important respect. Because money was so tight the refurnishing was minimal and many old items had to be reused. Hay's colour schemes normally took their starting point in the textiles but such new carpets and curtains as had to be supplied were far from luxurious. By the time the watercolours were taken, however, conditions had ameliorated but the eccentricity of the rooms had been aggravated by the introduction of continental exhibition pieces.

Hay had a freer hand in Prince Albert's Drawing Room which had the smallest area of panelling. The

31

31d

31e

richness of its colouring arises from the deliberate contrast between its crimson walls and the olive curtains. These have been harmonised by the large areas of tertiary colour on the framework of the ceiling. The room has been unified by repeating the contrasting colours on the flat of the ceiling and the curtain trimmings. The watercolour cannot recapture the subtlety of Hay's effects which derived from his mastery of his raw material, paint. His ceilings were painted with colours fixed in turpentine rather than oil which gave a 'fresco-like effect' of 'aerial lightness'. The ceiling was further enriched by stencilled gilding incorporating the royal monograms. In the other rooms the ceilings pick up the tones of the panelling and tapestry but the colours introduced are balanced with Hay's meticulous care creating

a unified effect throughout the Royal Apartment.

Under Matheson's direction, improvements continued but there was never the money that the Palace deserved and whole areas, like the Picture Gallery, remained derelict. In 1856 a small sum was granted to refit the Throne Room which had been last decorated for George IV in 1822. Its use as the Throne Room enshrined the purely temporary arrangements that prevailed on that occasion and it had actually been intended as the Carolean Guard Chamber which is why it had never received a ornamental ceiling. To supply this deficiency Matheson designed a boldly projecting heraldic ceiling illustrating the descent of the Stewarts which was intended to 'accord' with the others in the 'continuous suite'. Although Matheson had been severely repri-

31f

manded in 1850 for permitting Hay to supply ornamental work which was 'not charged', it is difficult to believe that the leading craftsman of Edinburgh did not resort to the same methods in 1856 to ensure that Scotland's premier interior should be worthy of its lofty purpose in spite of London's parsimony. The ceiling was modelled by John Ramage and Son who also created the richly undercut cornice which incorporates the thistle, the lily, the shamrock and the rose. The resplendent paper in crimson, gold and blue was probably supplied by William McCrie, Scotland's leading paper-stainer while the grate, with its thistles and lion rampant, was manufactured by James Gray. The paintwork was executed by David Ramsay Hay who finished the ceiling in imitation of oak with full heraldic tinctures and the ribs were outlined in crimson to unify the scheme. There was no question of supplying a new throne, so George IV's (which was actually his mother, Queen Charlotte's, canopy and chair from her Saloon at Buckingham house) was spruced up. The dignity of the refitted room was somewhat diminished by the necessity of it having to continue to double up as the Royal Dining Room, such was the shortage of space at the Palace.

31g

The Queen's return to Holyrood made it a centre of public attention and led to a growing desire for visits by a curious public. In 1852 the Lord Provost of Edinburgh petitioned the Queen with the request that Holyrood might be opened along similar lines to Hampton Court. The matter was referred to the Commissioners of Works, and their Principal Architect in Scotland, Robert Matheson, probably in collusion with the Lord Provost undertook the arrangements enthusiastically. The greatest public interest lay in Queen Mary's rooms and Matheson satisfied his colleagues that they could be given independent access and the necessary doors locked to separate them from the areas used by the Queen and her household. In a sense the state was merely regularising the existing arrangements operated for their personal profit by the Duke of Hamilton's servants. The smoothness of the transition owed everything to the fact that the Duke's housekeeper, Mrs Quinet, was eighty-three years old and had devoted twenty-eight of these years to this focal point of Scotland's expanding tourist trade. She was persuaded to retire, but not before she had personally petitioned the Queen on behalf of the 'two fatherless grandchildren' whose education had been financed by the tourists' tips and with the request to be permitted to 'end her days' in her apartments at the Palace.

Fortunately the proposed new arrangements did not affect the Chapel Royal which had been efficiently shown for many years by David Anderson, as the many editions of his guidebook show and who would undoubtedly have proved a more difficult task to dislodge. Matheson was insistent that Mrs Quinet and her female servants should be replaced by men and, with great tact, he asked the Duke to make the appointments. William Ross was appointed keeper of Queen Mary's Rooms. The new proposals had required the Duke vacate his first floor rooms which were now added to the newly christened 'Historical Apartments'. The first floor rooms became rather fancifully known as the 'Darnley Apartments' and placed under the supervision of Peter Gray. It was only after the men had taken over that Matheson discovered that he now had nobody to carry out the work of housekeeping and so female cleaners were hurriedly appointed. The rooms were opened at sixpence per ticket on five days of the week but Saturday opening was free. The admission figures showed that Holyrood was soon established as a popular revenue-earning, attraction. An early stereoscopic photograph reveals the elaborate barriers introduced by the Matheson to keep the public away from the precious relics and shows that the room took photography in its stride proving, indeed, unusually photogenic. In 1864, Matheson presented estimates for the repair of the Historical apartments. These proposed a thorough overhaul of the panelling, the open joints of which were to be stopped, and the removal of the prominent damp stains on Queen Mary's Bedroom ceiling. The existing 'stone' coloured paint was to be replaced by a uniform coat of graining 'in imitation of old oak', to play up the antiquarian effect. At the same time the silk hangings of the Supper Room which were 'falling in pieces' were to be 'taken dawn and the remains carefully preserved'. It was also noted that 'Queen Mary's apartments contain prints of a comparatively recent date and of an inferior character which shall be taken off the walls'.

Matheson was now, unwittingly, poised on a very slippery slope. Since in fact almost nothing in the rooms was genuine, the gradual removal of the dubious was to climax, during the early 1980s, in the destruction of the rooms themselves. Also, the visual impact of the rooms had depended for its success on the exaggerated state of decay vividly captured in Swarbreck's lithographs. After their sprucing-up the underfurnished look of the Darnley Apartment must have become very obvious. Happily, however, the opportunity arose at this very moment – doubtless arranged by Matheson himself – for the state to acquire an important collection of furniture 'from the Royal Palaces of Scotland', assembled by R. G. Ellis, an Edinburgh lawyer, who wished to see it preserved at Holyrood. This remarkable group of furnishings was reported to be the fruit of '20 or 30 years of labour' and it is surprising to learn that all the items shared only three provenances – the Royal Palaces of Holyrood, Falkland and Dunfermline with the exception of a chair from Glasgow Cathedral. The collection was favourably vetted by W. B. Johnstone, Curator of the National Gallery and who, as an artist, would have been conversant with this kind of item as studio props for history pictures. Part of the collection was acquired for £300, but only after a certain amount of haggling during which Ellis was reminded that both the honour of seeing his collection in a 'National Museum' and the pleasure that the collecting must have afforded him was more than compensation for the loss of £200 from his valuation.

Matheson was also able to acquire a large quantity of tapestry from Ellis and in addition to the now famous set of 'Playing Boys' there was enough to line the closets of 'Darnley's' bedroom and thus expunge the last vestiges of the Hamilton's modish but now glaringly anachronistic paperhangings. In 1868, following the death of Johnstone, the sale of his possessions gave Matheson the opportunity to acquire further allegedly Royal Scottish

furniture. In 1874, in spite of a tight budget, he was able to bid successfully at the J. N. Paton sale in Dunfermline [25] and thus the kitchen grate from the Palace there came to Holyrood. Surprisingly the state's supervision of these rooms did not lead to any critical analysis of the basis of their presentation. Sadly no catalogue of the expanding collection was prepared and, if anything, confusion multiplied when the crimson velvet bed was moved down a floor to Darnley's rooms and its long association with Charles I was thus automatically replaced by an even more improbable identification with Darnley. In the process the one fact that was remembered about it – its use by Bonnie Prince Charlie – seems to have been forgotten.

33: THE DRAWING ROOM AT 9 DICK PLACE, EDINBURGH
1861

This lively watercolour offers a rare glimpse of one of the interiors of the growing number of villas to the south of Edinburgh whose colonisation of the countryside was to be so roundly condemned by Robert Louis Stevenson 'as belonging to no style of art, only to a form of business much to be regretted'.

The standard pattern for these villas was to have the bay-windowed Drawing Room on the first floor directly above the ground floor Dining Room. As can be seen, the drawing room is contained within the gable of the roof, probably not so much for Picturesque external effect as to cut costs. The room has a standard slab-format white Grecian chimneypiece but again, to keep costs down, this seems to be veined rather than the purest statuary marble. The furniture is smart and probably as new as the house. It is remarkable for its highly-sprung and over-buttoned comfort with luxuriant rolls on the backrest of the couch. In the left hand corner a heavily carved Jacobean style oak bookcase is just visible and is similar to that at Warriston [27] suggesting that this was a fashionable look. To modern eyes the strangest feature is the way the curtain rod cuts off the bay window rather than following its recess, but this seems to have been a standard treatment in Edinburgh villas. The bay furnished with a wire stand filled with flowering plants thereby assumed a conservatory look. The plush table cover is probably of Richard Whytock's patent velvet pile the pattern being printed before making up.

The Balmoral estate once formed part of the lands purchased in 1730 by William Duff, a successful entrepreneur, who invested his profits in properties confiscated from exiled Jacobites. His family subsequently claimed the Earldom of Fife. They built a neat Georgian shooting box, Mar Lodge, on the banks of the Dee at the head of the valley. Unfortunately the Lodge was flooded in the 'Muckle Spate' of 1828 and a new house was economically constructed on a safe eminence nearby. It was christened Corriemulzie Cottage, from a neighbouring burn. The modesty of the new house soon proved insufficient for the accommodation of the large numbers of visitors drawn by the growing popularity of Deeside. The Cottage, which was often let, was gradually expanded in a series of additions creating a glorified shack, charitably described in Groome's *Gazetteer* as a 'rambling structure between a Swiss Chalet and an Indian Bungalow'.

These marked architectural failings, however, proved to be the source of its very considerable charms, and after the sale of Balmoral to the Queen, the Fifes' tenants found themselves entertaining the sovereign, as their neighbour, in this enchanting hut. These photographs were taken by Victor Albert Prout in 1863 as part of a record of a series of charades performed in the presence of the Prince and Princess of Wales. The view of the Drawing Room confirms the simplicity of the structure with its plain cornice and marblised wood chimneypiece. A light scheme of decoration has been chosen which the design pundits would have approved as being suitable to a country residence. The moiré wallpaper reflected current fashion and its broad botanical

34a

border has been imaginatively repeated to frame the chimney-glass. The same pretty floral chintz has been used for both the curtains and the permanent loose-covers. The furniture is simple and the tables have painted legs and cloth tops the fringes of which are repeated on the shelves and chimney-shelf. The distinctive Deeside contribution to this relaxed decor, whose languor has infected its occupants, comes in the massed ranks of stags' heads. The idea of a metal armature to produce an erect head was a later innovation, so this herd looks dolefully into the carpet. In the Dining Room, whose top-lighting reflects the house's architec-

tural innocence, the massed ranks of antlers are positively threatening. The fleur-de-lis carpet, where propriety would have demanded a Turkey rug, is another sign of the prevailing informality. The table setting has almost as much game as the walls and chimney-shelf. In 1889 the connection between the Fifes and their Royal neighbours was sealed when Princess Louise, daughter of the Prince of Wales, married the Earl of Fife who was granted a Dukedom. Corriemulzie Cottage was deemed an unsuitable residence for a future Princess Royal and a new Mar Lodge arose, to the designs of Marshall Mackenzie of Aberdeen.

34b

Early views of Glasgow town houses are so rare that it comes as no surprise to discover that the earliest photographs have as their subject the city's most opulent terraced house. No. 52 (originally No. 8) Carlton Place was built by the merchant, John Laurie, for his own occupation. In its extravagance there was an element of both self-advertisment and the show-house, Carlton Place being but one part of Laurie's extensive property developments over the land in the Gorbals which he had purchased in 1801. With his enthusiasm for attracting attention to himself, Laurie was to prove an ideal patron for his architect, Peter Nicholson, who was clearly given an all too obviously free hand, a generous budget and an instruction to startle fellow Glaswegians.

Inevitably such an approach was inimicable to quiet good taste, and No. 52 exemplifies the very different spirit abroad in entrepreneurial Glasgow when compared to the desire for careful professional conformity which dominated the New Town of Edinburgh. Nicholson was a brilliant architect and seized his chance to turn the staircase into a dazzling spatial sequence, set off by luxuriant plasterwork. Nicholson is best remembered today for his extensive architectural publications which reveal the close critical attention that he exercised on every aspect of design and construction. No. 52 also displayed his technical advances, including a mechanical mode of holding the drawing room floors under tension for dancing. Laurie's satisfaction with his architect was given handsome expression when he named one of the new streets in the Gorbals after him. The importance of these photographs is greatly increased because they can be related both to an inventory of the house taken in 1817 and to visitors' published descriptions.

At first sight the drawing room is a rare record of the stiff formality of fashionable metropolitan practice as codified in Sheraton's celebrated engraving of a drawing room published in 1793 with which Laurie was fully familiar. Comparison between the Inventory and the photograph reveals that the set of light, round-backed, 'painted and gilt' chairs were original to the room and the 'painted and gilt' cabinet between the doors comprised part of the same suite. Some of chairs and the commode remain in their original position around the the perimeter of the room. The arm of one of the two

original 'couches' on either side of the chimneypiece, behind the camera, can just be seen at the bottom of the photograph. However, the room has been softened to bring it into line with more recent ideas through the addition of the two fully upholstered chairs, one of which, in the Elizabethan style, has Berlin woolwork upholstery. These innovations were probably not only intended to promote greater comfort but also deliberately to break up the stylistic unity of the original effect. The what-not which interrupts the line of chairs has the same purpose, but the round loo table has been introduced in response to the new fashion for centre tables. The 'mahogany Sofa Table' behind the Elizabethan chair, appears in the inventory but has now, at least for the photographer's temporary purposes, found a new role as a subsidiary centre-table bearing an appropriate weight of elegantly-bound and fashionable drawing room literature for visitors to peruse. The rococo revival carpet looks like a further part of the secondary refurnishing campaign and in 1817 the room had a 'Wilton carpet' and 'calico' curtains. Because silk curtains were the norm for grand drawing rooms the 'calico' must surely have been raised to the appropriate standard by means of an elaborate printed design testifying to the vitality of the local textile manufacturers. The upholstery of the seat furniture is sadly not specified in the Inventory but appears to bear no pattern and has the sheen of a velvet pile, then an unusual choice for a drawing room. The use of wallpaper, however, was the convention for town drawing rooms.

The garniture of the commode is an arresting feature. The two Michelangelesque vases, fitted with candle branches, the clock and possibly the small vase were all in the room by 1817: '2 bronze Vases, 1 cup and 1 shell, 1 8-day clock and glass cover'. Their very formal composition is in line with the original character of the room. The 'large lustre suspended from ceiling' was original and does not seem to have been adapted for gas when the scrolled brackets were added to the organ-case.

If the drawing room's contents broadly conformed to fashionable norms, its general tone was self-consciously unconventional. The profusion of plasterwork, underlined in the unusually deep frieze allowing plenty of space for the spread of the cornucopia, has few parallels in Scottish towns and its nearest peers are in Dublin. The showy Gothic organ is a further aspect of conspicuous consumption. Its two stools were mentioned in 1817 and are *en suite* with the seat furniture and commode whose open fretwork may have been intended to complement the case. Although the cabinet pictures comprising 'landscapes', 'Historical pieces', 'l Dutch painting' and a 'Cattle piece' are standard drawing room fare, the full-length 'Family paintings' were surely extraordinary in such an apartment and fit their places on either side of the organ so neatly that they must have been especially commissioned.

Although dining rooms were normally fitted up in a lower key than drawing rooms, Laurie's guests can have felt no sense of diminution of ornament as they processed down Nicholson's intricate staircase with its startling vistas through the house to the dining room where there is the same spirit of straining to be bigger and better. In Edinburgh, as at Warriston [27] recessed plaster panelling was fashionable for dining rooms, but no Modern Athenian could have contemplated commissioning this spread of plaster ornament. Elspeth Gallie, who wrote two pioneering articles on No. 52 Carlton

Place during the 1950s, when its future was under threat, suggested that the plasterer might have been Bernasconi because there was a tradition that the craftsman had worked at Windsor Castle. It certainly has a virtuoso flair with exceptionally fine figurative roundels. Elspeth Gallie also published an account of a visitor to the house recording that the dining room walls were 'distempered' with a 'salmon tint' and the photograph certainly reveals some picking out in colour but, sadly, cannot confirm the same visitor's impression that the 'rich floral decoration' surrounding the roundels was 'tinted in natural colours'. The photograph does show that Nicholson's handsome chimneypiece was in a dark marble, and black was rapidly established as the norm in dining rooms although not even D. R. Hay's books on colour theory reveal why this choice seemed so obvious at the time. The sombre tonality is continued by mahogany doors and, given Glasgow's prominence as an importer of American timbers, they were more likely to have been in solid mahogany than mere imitation graining. (In the Edinburgh dining room of the furniture maker, William Trotter, the doors are of the finest cabinet-veneers of fiddle-back mahogany.) The carpet is

35a

in the conventional Turkey pattern, but since the original carpet of 1817 was described as an 'old Wilton' this may be a more recent replacement.

If the components of the suite of furniture are standard, their ornamental splendour was fully in keeping with the spirit of the house and were far more massive than anything supplied by Trotter for his Edinburgh customers. The sideboard is fitted to its curved recess and has the standard Scottish superstructure with a sliding tambour front, but its fat fluted legs seem oversubstantial, even given the necessity of their supporting the 'two bronze statues' which are surely of painted plaster. Not the least arresting features to late twentieth-century eyes in this dining room photograph must be the less theatrical details which had parallels in more modest homes. The 'patent bronze lamp' in the centre of the sideboard like the '2 black figures with branches' on the chimneypiece would have been the conventional norm for lighting dining rooms. The '2 hand screens' decoratively displayed on the chimneypiece are also recorded in the Inventory, but the vases filling the void below the sideboard are later introductions although such an arrangement was common. In 1817 the curtains were of red moreen and the room contained a number of small tables and a music stand suggesting that it also functioned as the family's 'ordinary' evening sitting room. The upholstery of the chairs is horsehair, deep-buttoned on the voluptuous arm chairs. The high gloss on the furniture must be the result of varnish but the highly prized glassy surface of the dinner table must be the result of continual labour and constant vigilance. In her reminiscences of her early life in the New Town of Edinburgh, Mrs Story writes vividly of the bustle that heralded dinner parties when two Highland caddies would be drafted in to hand-burnish the dinner tables to the requisite gloss.

Laurie's Trustees sold his house in the early 1860s and these photographs may have been commissioned at this time as a deliberate record. Unusually there are no flowers in the drawing room for the photographic session and the photographer seems to have been at pains to bring the rooms to life by setting the furniture at Picturesque angles to his lens, while the still life on the dinner table with its ink standish and folded newspaper belongs firmly to the cult of the 'lived in look'.

35b

36: THREE VICTORIAN DRAWING ROOMS, AT AUCHINLECK, LAURENCEPARK HOUSE AND MAVISBANK HOUSE
c.1870

It is revealing that once the technical problems of recording interiors had been mastered, the first subjects requested from the Victorian photographer were almost all drawing rooms. In all three of these houses, the drawing room was the only one that was deemed worthy of a photograph.

This vivid record of the trappings of a Louis Revival Drawing Room was probably incidental to the photographer's purpose because the prime focus of his attention must have been the Boswell family's armorial crest over the central niche [36a]. As a result of the fame of James Boswell's biography of Dr Johnson, Auchinleck became a literary shrine. Johnson had visited Boswell at his family home but he preferred the 'sullen dignity of the old castle' to 'the elegance of the modern mansion' which they had built c.1765 to replace it. Characteristically, its largest room was the Great Dining Room whose

most prominent feature was a Buffet niche for the display of plate. In its conversion to a Victorian Drawing Room, the niche lost its shelves to become a receptacle for the statue. Its elaborate stucco flourishes have all but vanished into the camouflage provided by the busy wallpaper which has been meticulously cut around the plaster rinceau. The principal furnishings of sofa, pier tables with glasses and gilt curtain boxes are all in a markedly Louis style with reversing 'C' scrolls expensively carved, but it is interesting that the pier table on the right has been bodged-up to provide a pair to that on the left and their glasses do not seem to match either. The sofa's upholstery with its pleats and diminutive buttoning is quite as elaborate as the complexities of the pelmets with their ropes and bugle fringing. The woodwork, including the doors reflected in the glasses and the plaster framework of the niche have all been grained

36a

· 88 ·

and high-varnished. The carpet pattern seems to consist of realistically shaded bows of ribbon with a deep border and would have upset the design reformers of Edinburgh because of unsuitability for a flat surface. The three japanned papier-maché chairs of different patterns in the foreground, like the pair of gilt-wood ones, must have been positioned to overcome the photographer's dislike of empty space. It would be fascinating to know where the furnishings hailed from and, if it was Glasgow, they certainly contrast with the relative repose of Trotter's Mavisbank Drawing Room [36c]. A set of effective wooden Venetian blinds protected the textiles from the sun's destructive rays.

Laurencepark is a Tudor revival villa which was possibly designed by the Edinburgh architect, Thomas Hamilton. This photograph [36b] may record an interior scheme by David Ramsay Hay. In composing his decorations, Hay payed great attention to a room's aspect and function. The pale tones and chintz curtains would have been deemed suitable for a summer residence whereas a more 'substantial' style would have demanded that the compartment ceiling should be oak grained and that the curtains of a drawing room should be of silk. Hay's scientific approach led to his hatred of wallpaper. In the damp Scottish climate paper became liable to 'putrefaction' and filled a room with 'the effluvia from the decayed animal and vegetable substances necessarily employed in this mode of decoration'. His solution was to oil paint the walls and stencil them with geometric patterns in gold, which in grand houses would quote from the family's heraldry. The careful spacing of the motifs here confirms that this cannot be a paper. Hay thought up endless variations on this theme and his schemes often included textured effects producing imitations of damask hangings or gold embroideries. The techniques required considerable dexterity with the stencils some of which must have been on a large scale although the pattern shown here must have been relatively easy to execute.

Hay's books are amongst the earliest writings to condemn loud floral carpets as a disturbing influence in the composition of a room In his colour schemes even the

36b

cover of the ubiquitous centre-table had to harmonise and here it appears to be in a velvet pile. It was probably made by Richard Whytock of Edinburgh who had first applied the technique of printing his patterns prior to weaving in the manufacture of the cheap printed carpets which made his fortune. Whytock was one of the first manufacturers to employ a resident artist-designer, winning Hay's confidence and full approval.

During the second quarter of the nineteenth century, Sir John Clerk of Penicuik's Baroque villa of Mavisbank house was converted into a larger country house by the addition of lateral wings, and the piano nobile was transferred from the first to the ground floor. The additions may have been carried out for George Clerk Arbuthnot who had purchased the house from Graeme Mercer in 1842. This sumptuous Drawing Room occupied one of the new pavilions. The importance of this photograph derives from its upholsterer rather than from the unknown architect. In 1986 the

36c

National Monuments Record of Scotland acquired two albums of designs by Trotter, Edinburgh's leading furniture maker, which include the design for the side wall of this room showing the curtain boxes, pier glasses and acanthus scroll pier tables. This is therefore a rare illustration of the firm's best work and it displays a fascinating blend of restrained grandeur with practical comfort, as one might expect from such a long established and experienced firm. William Trotter had died in 1833 but the firm was continued as the 'Heirs of Mr Trotter' until Charles, who was only seventeen when his father died, was old enough to assume full control.

The restraint of the furniture also extends to the room as a whole and there is a uniform tonality between the walls and the ceiling as advocated by D. R. Hay in his writings on interior decoration. The gilt pattern on the walls suggest that they are painted with one of his many variations on his patent textured paints which imitated flock effects. The coffers of the curved ceiling vault appear to be tinted in colour behind the rosettes which was a method of unifying the colour-scheme throughout a room recommended by Hay. The fringed pelmets with a deep bugle fringe, whose silk hangers are wound round wooden moulds, seem to have been popular in Scotland. The silk damask curtains have an applied border with anthemion ornaments. The same damask appears to be used to cover the two chairs which, typically, are of different styles and the fully stuffed sofa looks remarkably comfortable. The most important pieces of furniture are the mirror backed chiffoniers. The Trotter albums contain working drawings for similar cabinets and doubtless the ormolu mounts were subcontracted. The room contains characteristic groupings of furniture including a grand piano with round music stool, a centre table and ottoman, a sofa table and three of a set of curved back sidechairs undoubtedly in a fine cabinet-wood. The embroidered cloth-covered table must be of colonial manufacture and has a Far Eastern table-cover. The magnificent 'Louis' carpet must have been especially made for the room. Trotter's best-recorded late commission is Crom Castle in Northern Ireland where the carpets were especially made in London but that may have been by the client's choice. Certainly Richard Whytock's factory at nearby Lasswade could weave knotted carpets of drawing room quality as they did for Lennox Castle. The room is lit by candles and is enlivened through the lavish use of flowers and plants.

These photographs come from a sumptuous red morocco album bearing 'The Cairns 1858' in gilt on the front cover. However, a later inscription records that it was presented 'To Mrs J. P. Kidston with Mr Burnet's Compliments September 1875'. It was probably originally bound up to contain photographs, by Annan, of the architect John Burnet's designs for the Kidston's Baronial villa. The interior and exterior photographs show the house as well established, rather than newly built, and they must have been added nearer the time of the presentation. Kidston was a coal master and the furnishings and decoration of the villa reflect his prosperity. The photographs betray a fascinating tension between their architectural decorations and the contents which, when compared with the succeeding illustrations of Alexander 'Greek' Thomson's contemporary villa interiors, show that Glasgow's architects were experimenting with interior design at this time. Burnet created an ingeniously intricate entrance to the house, passing through a double Gothic arch supported by a highly polished marble pillar, opening into the Staircase Hall. Stained glass, Minton tiles and a pair of copies of the famous Glastonbury chairs complemented its ecclesiastic decorations but the dinner-gong belongs resolutely to the middle of the nineteenth century.

The Drawing Room reveals the typical muddle of styles common at this date. Burnet followed through the Baronial style of his exterior with a trabeated ceiling of plaster beams imitating timber. However, this has not been painted up in antiquarian taste with oak graining but has been left in a pale flat shade. Perhaps, like Laurencepark [36b], this was because The Cairns was

37a

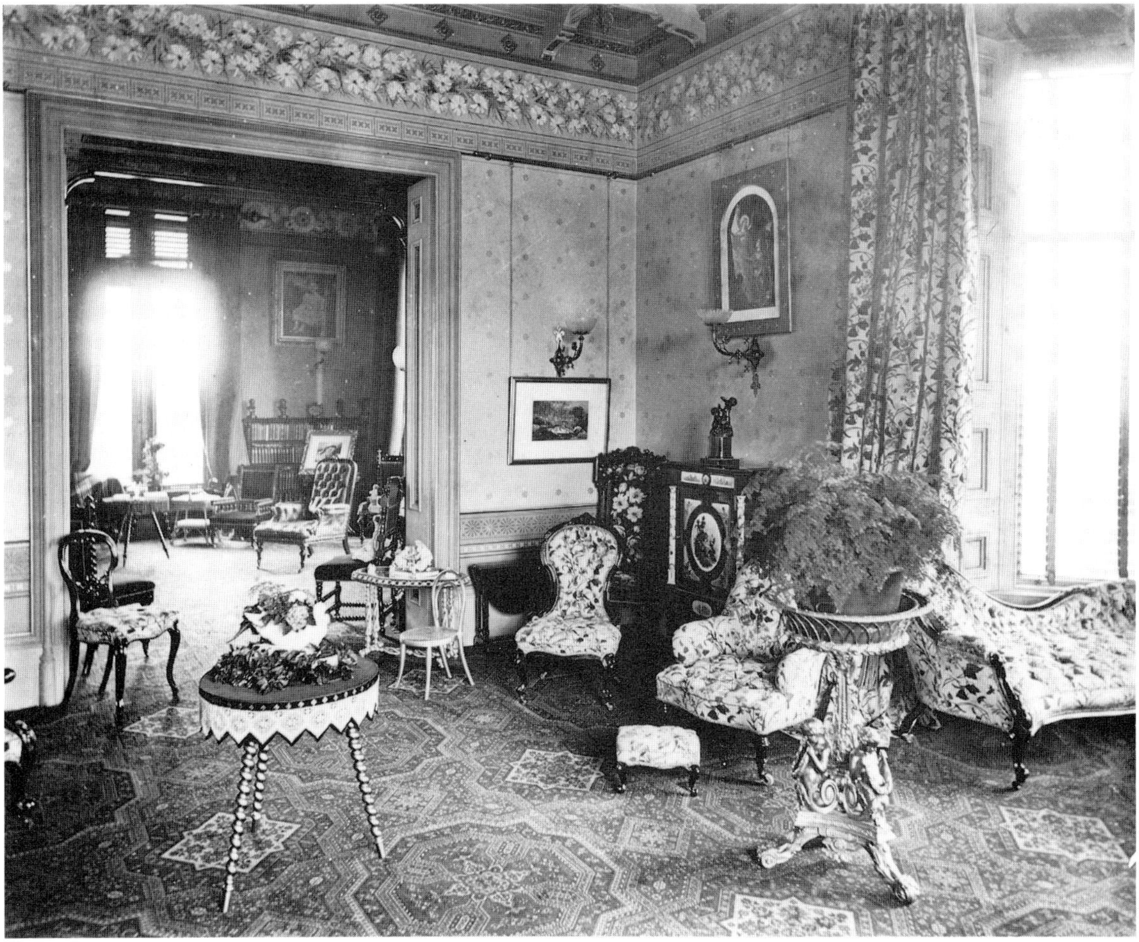

37c

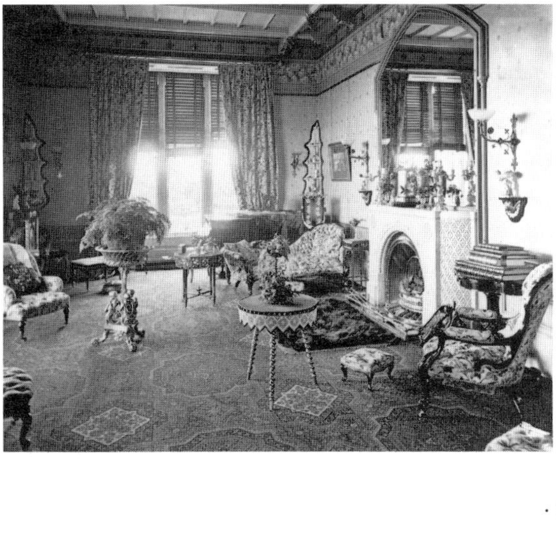

37b

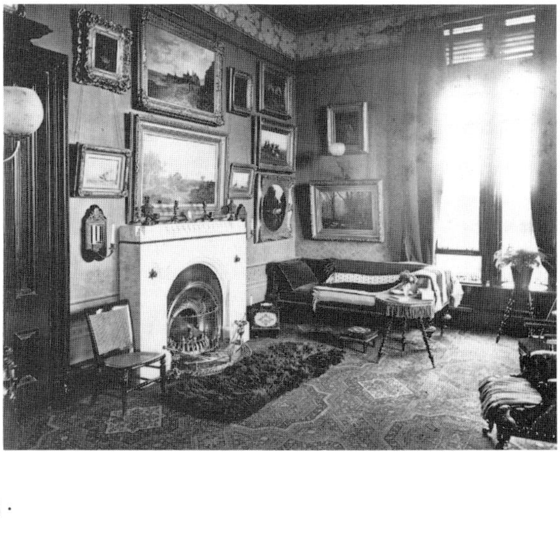

37d

intended to function as a summer residence. The Baronial theme is continued with a Gothic chimney-glass. Although this is integrated with the chimney-piece by the attached colonettes, the two are in markedly different styles. Burnet must have designed the highly imaginative statuary marble chimney-piece himself. The glass also cuts awkwardly across the frieze in a way which suggests the lack of a single controlling hand. This division of the wall-face into different bands is a new element in decoration because the late-Georgian ideal had been an unbroken expanse of wallpaper between skirting and cornice. The skirting here is very deep and is surmounted by a broad band of stencilled ornament. Although the middle zone of stencilled gilt rosettes are familiar from D. R. Hay's work, the frieze above the picture rail is a novelty whose naturalistic flowers impart a fresh note to the room. The furniture, by contrast, was in a conventional Louis style, doubtless in a fancy cabinet wood. The chintz curtains and upholstery, where silk would be the norm for drawing rooms, were probably also intended to reflect the character of a summer residence. The suite was complemented by a pair of costly cabinets with porcelain plaques and colonettes which, unlike the Scottish seat furniture, are surely genuinely Parisian. The geometric Persian pattern of the carpet, used throughout the public rooms, would have satisfied design reformers who felt that carpets, like wallpapers, should have flat patterns, but this improving carpet seems ill at ease with some of the flashier Drawing Room gee-gaws such as the jardinière with its fern.

Although the Library inter-communicates with the Drawing Room through double sliding-doors, in keeping with Victorian ideas on the hierarchy of furnishings, it is in a much more sober Neo-Renaissance style with plush rather than chintz upholstery. The frieze here was almost ethnic in character with overtones of Polynesian feather-work. The walls had a less elaborate stencilled scheme in keeping with the display of the fairly serious looking collection of modern pictures. The Dining Room was fitted up in an extremely elaborate Jacobean style harmonising with the Baronial exterior and having a frieze of heraldic shields. The chimney-piece and furniture apparently *en suite* and therefore must have been designed as a unit by Burnet who failed to exert the same control in the Drawing Room. Each wall had a central feature. A large linen-fold sideboard stood opposite the chimney-piece with massive columnar legs matching those of the chimney-piece. Opposite the large window was a further linen-fold cabinet with columns which undoubtedly held the extra leaves for the extending telescopic dinner table. The family bible lay on top ready for family prayers and the inspiring painting above may have been deliberately placed as a focus for the same purpose. The walls of the Dining Room have been decorated with applied vertical lines, doubtless in contrasting colours. The Cairns must have been an important commission for Burnet as the preparation of this sumptuous album proves. The house was burnt by vandals after the last war and not even a gate-pier survives to prove its existence.

37e

37f

38: ALEXANDER 'GREEK' THOMSON'S VILLA INTERIORS
1868

Although very different in character from the surrounding illustrations, these plates depicting interiors by the Glasgow architect, Alexander 'Greek' Thomson (1817–75) from *Villa and Cottage Architecture*, 1876, are faithful records of his executed schemes rather than unrealised ideal designs. The book was a compendium of designs by British architects illustrating a deliberately varied range of examples. It was intended not only to help potential villa dwellers gauge the probable cost of their future home but also to encourage them to employ an architect by exposing the dangers of relying on a builder. Scotland was so well represented in the selection that a glossary of Scottish building terms had to be included. Thomson's plans, in comparison with the others, reveal an unusual interest in interior design. His innovations demonstrate the existence of a climate of experimental patronage in Glasgow at this time and the vitality of the tradesmen who carried them out. The

value of the plates is increased by lengthy letterpress descriptions which must have been supplied by the architects themselves. The close chronological juxtaposition of two of Thomson's designs, the Double Villa at Langside of 1856–7 and Holmwood at Cathcart of 1857–8, show Thomson evolving his philosophy of interior design with the benefit of a larger budget for the latter.

It is typical of the rigour of Thomson's approach that because the exteriors were styled in 'an adaptation of the Greek', their interiors had to harmonise. The section of the Langside villa [38a] reveals much careful rethinking of every aspect of domestic detailing in its Dining Room which is immediately noticeable in the joinery of the doors. The proportion of the doors seems to have provided Thomson with a module for his revived 'post and lintel' interior format and they were provided with columns supporting a frieze. This system was repeated throughout the room, creating a wall division that prefig-

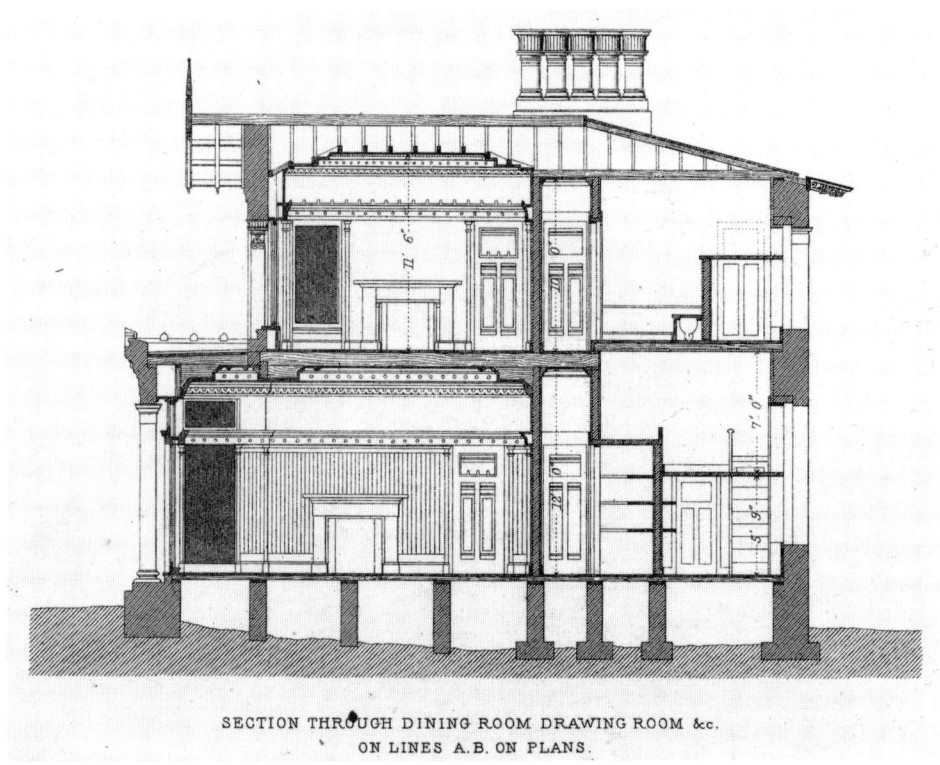

SECTION THROUGH DINING ROOM DRAWING ROOM &c.
ON LINES A.B. ON PLANS.

38a

ured the late-Victorian fondness for deep friezes. The windows were equal in size to the doors with their own colonettes supporting the frieze and creating an upper attic tier of windows. This upper register was of fixed lights and the Introduction to *Villa and Cottage Architecture* reveals that they were filled with coloured glass. The lower lights were sashes but Thomson had also rethought the pulley system and his sashes were able to travel both up, and down, giving great flexibility in ventilation. Space was left behind the colonettes for the 'working of blinds and curtains', instead of the upholsterer having to make the best of an architect's bad job, as was more usually the case.

The windows of the upstairs Drawing Room were French casements enabling the flat roof over the Dining Room's bay window to function as a balcony. While the frieze was plastered, the lower zone of the wall was lined out with vertical planks of 'yellow pine varnished' and 'preserving its natural colour and markings'. This was relieved in the Drawing Room by applied fret-work ornaments in mahogany glued on. This apparently rational design was justified, surprisingly, in visual terms:

> *The object of this mode of treatment is to unite together the several parts of the room, thereby giving an effect of increased extent. The apparent height of ceiling is also enhanced by giving force to the lower mass of the walls, and so making them serve as does a foreground to a picture.*

The larger budget at Holmwood [38b] gave Thomson the opportunity to develop these ideas to luxurious effect but the plates cannot recapture one important element:

> *The details here, as well as those of the principal rooms, are precisely shown, – wanting however, the colour – which, in this house, plays an important part in the internal effect.*

The articulation of the rooms employed the same system but the greater ceiling heights meant that Holmwood lacked the clarity of Langside in spite of devices like the introduction of a deep skirting. The spiky detail is extensively illustrated and reveals Thomson's total control. The widespread use of stencilling, which may have been in gold, is very much in the tradition of D. R. Hay's experiments during the 1830s. The decoration of

Holmwood, however, aspires to art. The Dining Room frieze reproduced Flaxman's 'illustrations of the Iliad' with the figures coloured brown on a blue ground and 'sharply defined in outline' while the panels of the upstairs Drawing Room, painted by the young artist, Hugh Cameron, were inspired by Tennyson's 'Idylls of the King'. Both Flaxman and Tennyson were held in high regard by Thomson.

The interiors were distinguished by a highly architectural approach to furnishings. The Dining Room had a fixed marble sideboard in a recess lined with mirrors emblazoned with gilt ornaments and framed in rosewood. Thomson identified the circular bay of the parlour as 'a fitting spot in which to establish the ladies' work-table' and the Hall had a 'recess for the hat-stand'. This precision-placing culminated in the Drawing Room where the centre of every wall had a special feature. Opposite the chimney-piece was the piano with a mirror over it, while opposite the window was 'another large mirror, with a decorated marble-slab in front supported by chimerae'. This must be the only mid-Victorian piano to have been treated as a significant architectural feature. Inevitably, 'Greek' Thomson favoured the slab-like marble chimney-pieces popularised by the earlier Greek Revival but these too were carefully rethought in his characteristic blend of the rational with the visual. By engraving their flat surfaces and gilding the incisions a brilliant effect resulted where:

> *The object in view, in adopting this mode of ornamentation, was to establish a harmony between the broad marble surfaces of the chimney-pieces and the decorated walls, and also with the various articles of taste usually arranged upon the mantel-shelf. Decoration in this manner can be executed at a very moderate cost when compared with carving in relief, seeing that there is much less work in producing the sunk cuttings, and that the thickness of marble required is but very little more than what is necessary for a plain chimney-piece.*

Sadly, nothing is known of the furniture of these rooms but Juliet Kinchin has found letters to *The Cabinet-maker*, a trade paper, which confirm that Thomson was equally interested in this area of interior decoration.

Overleaf: 38b

HOLMWOOD.
SECTIONS AND DETAILS.

Horizontal Sect

Elevation and Section
of Cornice &c. in Drawing Room

Elevation and Section
of Cornice &c. in Parlour

Section through Drawing Room and Parlour.

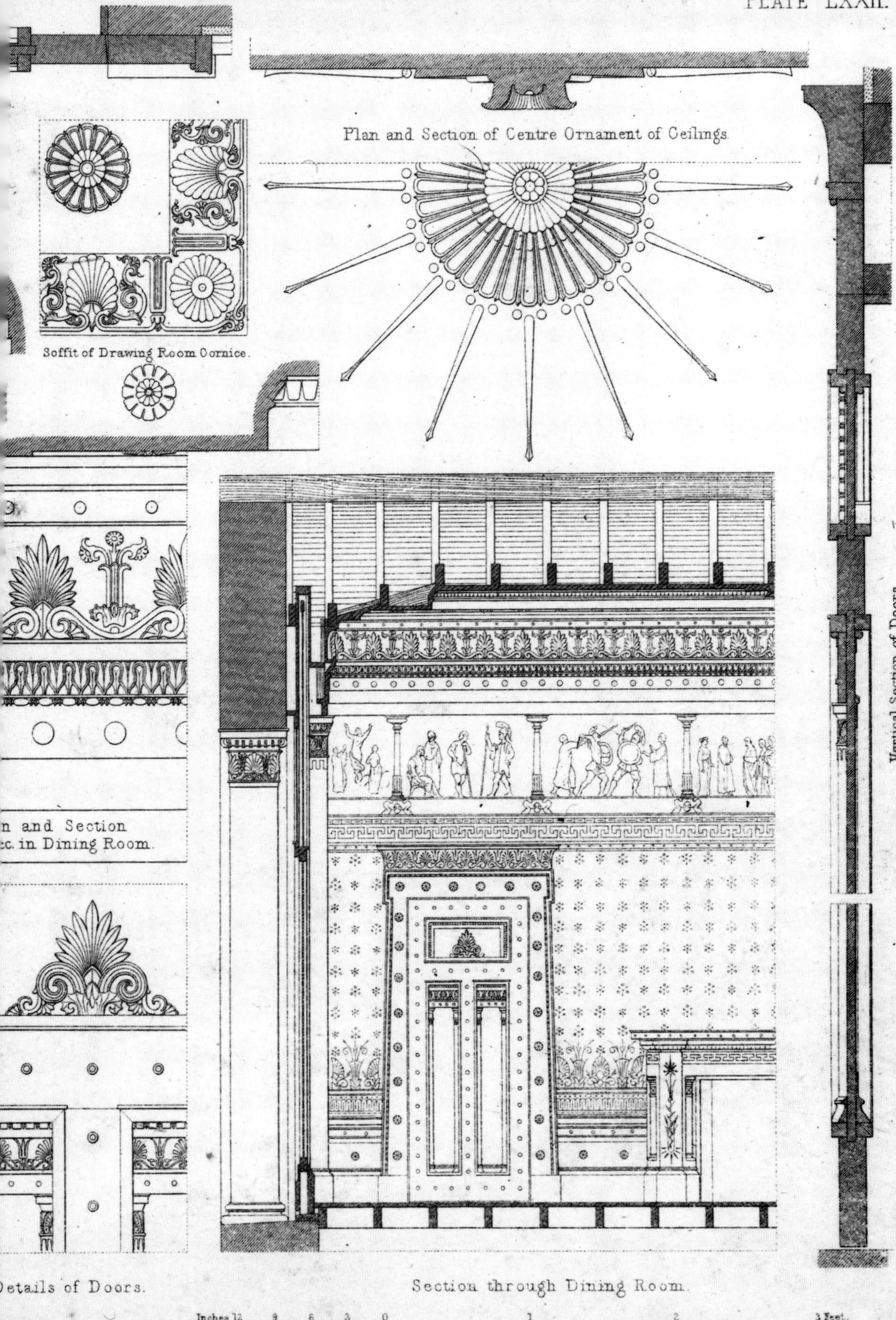

PLATE LXXII.

Plan and Section of Centre Ornament of Ceilings.

Soffit of Drawing Room Cornice.

n and Section
c. in Dining Room.

Vertical Section of Doors.

Details of Doors.

Section through Dining Room.

Blythswood was a magnificent Neo-Classical house built by Archibald Campbell, MP for Glasgow, to the designs of James Gillespie Graham in the early 1820s on the banks of the Clyde. With the rapid expansion and growing importance of the city during the late nineteenth century, Blythswood developed a new role as the Royal family's base for visits to Glasgow in much the same way as Dalkeith Palace had functioned for Edinburgh before Holyrood was restored. The historic importance of these visits led to a number of photographic records of the house and its interiors. The earliest seems to date from the visit of the Prince and Princess of Wales in 1876. The views of the Hall show the original decorative scheme with the walls lined out as ashlar blocks, the doors and woodwork grained and the columns marbled. The Drawing Room, however, must have been refitted about the middle of the century when it received a new

chimneypiece, an elaborately painted ceiling and silk panelled walls. The photograph of Queen Victoria's Bedroom dates from 1888, when she came to open the Glasgow Exhibition. The view shows an extraordinary confection of a chair with gilt and embroidery which is a vestige of the extravagant upholstery deemed suitable for Royal visits in previous centuries, whilst the sober bed is much more in the spirit of an engraving in the same room which showed the young Queen signing the oath of the Church of Scotland at her Accession. Comparison between the photographs also shows how the Drawing Room's contents were thinned down through a purge of its earlier Victorian contents in order to receive a fashionable Louis XVI stamp. The worktable with its lyre-shaped supports may be a survivor from the room's original contents.

39a

39c

39d

40: THE KITCHEN AT OLD CRICHIE HOUSE, ABERDEENSHIRE
1877

Illustrations of kitchens are so rare that this charming naïve watercolour is particularly welcome. All that is known about it is contained on the label attached to the frame: 'Interior of the Kitchen of Old Crichie House Mrs Walker sitting in the chimney and the maid at work 1877 by John S. Muir'. Although the scale is suspect, producing, as it does the rather surreal effect, like a setting from a fairy tale, it doubtless provides a faithful record of many aspects of the rural economy, including the fish-curing by the substantial fire and the hams suspended from the rafters. On the right hand side is a box bed and the chair on the far right has been painted green which seems to have been a common colour. This kitchen (unlike [47]) is hardly a promising Picturesque subject and sentiment must have been Muir's motivation in recording this familiar scene.

41: AN UNIDENTIFIED EDINBURGH NEW TOWN DRAWING ROOM
c.1880

It is always interesting to be able to see the full three hundred and sixty degrees of a room. These photographs show the persistence of the taste of the 1820s through the satinwood graining on the woodwork, the ottoman seats and the flock wallpaper with its narrow gilt fillet. The room has made some concessions to modern fashions, however, through the introduction of the seventeenth-century cabinet placed opposite the chimneypiece and the Charles II style chair. One of the ottomans has been displaced from the fireside to accommodate a Davenport desk and an ethnic rug has been thrown over the Grecian sofa on top of the matching chintz covers. The real change, however, lies in the plethora of framed paintings and drawings which are even hung densely across the folding doors to the Back Drawing Room. Their hanging suggests that the big doors were no longer used and this may indicate a typical rearrangement of the late-Georgian plan. One effect of the desire for a suite of identically furnished interconnecting Drawing Rooms on the first floor had been to push the master bedroom onto the ground floor. Many back drawing rooms were converted into bedrooms by their Victorian owners and the redundant folding doors were removed. Often an 'L'-shaped single drawing room resulted. The excessive ranks of pictures obviously represent a special enthusiasm but they may also indicate a tenant's attempt to force their personality onto a very old fashioned rented property.

41a

41b

42: THOMAS BONNAR II's
OWN DRAWING ROOM AT 7 ANN STREET, EDINBURGH
c.1880

Thomas Bonnar II was well qualified to lead the decorative art revival in Scotland. His grandfather was a well known Edinburgh house-painter who has assisted Alexander Runciman with the decoration of Penicuik House in the 1770s, his uncle William Bonnar was an early artist member of the Royal Scottish Academy and his aunt had married George Meikle Kemp, the celebrated architectural illustrator who also designed the Scott monument. Bonnar published a biography of Kemp in 1892. His father, Thomas Bonnar, was the finest decorative painter in Scotland who, after running the ornamental department of D. R. Hay and Co., left to set up in business with another of Hay's pupils, Robert Carfrae, much to their master's chagrin. After Hay's death in 1866, Bonnar and Carfrae became the leading decorators in Scotland, absorbing other long-established firms and enjoying the patronage of David Bryce, the leading architect of the period. Thomas II inherited the business on his father's death in 1873 and acted as its principal designer, bringing the fresh spirit of the aesthetic movement to the rooms decorated by the firm during the 1880s.

This photograph of his own Drawing Room must date from c.1880 because an illustration of the room appears in his presidential address to the Edinburgh Architectural Association [42c] which they published as *The Present Art Revival in Scotland* in 1879. No. 7 Ann Street was a typical later New Town house with plain Grecian detail. Although it was too severe for Bonnar's taste the fact that he left its architecture and even its bland chimney-piece untouched illustrates one of the tenets of his lecture which maintained that an art atmosphere could be infused into the dullest room through the introduction of skilfully selected colour, pattern and textiles and there was thus no necessity to discard all of a client's existing possessions as unscrupulous tradesmen were wont to do. Bonnar disliked fashionable one-period rooms and admired the Picturesque effect of old family houses. He particularly admired Barncluith, near Hamilton, and he illustrated a view of its panelled drawing room [42b] whose 'wonderful preservation' made it a 'fair example of what the houses of the gentry were in

the last century'. Through his description of its panelling, 'Chippendale' furniture and 'French tapestry', Bonnar seems to be conjuring up a Scottish version of the 'Queen Anne' style, but in his lecture, he also singles out for praise Queen Mary's Bed-Chamber at Holyrood to which he brought an uncritical decorator's eye.

Bonnar infused his own nineteenth-century drawing room with an eighteenth-century character through the addition of Adamesque festoons with vases to the cornice and the transformation of the wall-press into a glazed china-cabinet in the same style. This look was completed by Chippendale-style pier and chimney-glasses, and has been married to the more modern note struck by the geometric wallpapers whose high dado is marked by a band of embossed flowers and leaves in Japanoiserie taste. The wallpapers serve as a background for the judiciously arranged art collection whose frames have been arranged with a considerable concern for symmetry. The furniture is also in modern aesthetic style and the chairs have been derived from Empire models. The card-table against the pier with its platform base may be intended to be complementary. The art-cabinet, which was probably ebonised like the seat furniture, so precisely lines up on the upper dado fillet that it must have been planned. It supports a display of Chinamania which also spreads to the floor where the dark polished boards serve to set it off. Interestingly, Bonnar thought that this was an eighteenth-century effect but the area of bare boardage was also a reaction to the omnipresent fitted carpets of late Georgian and early Victorian drawing rooms. The lace curtains, whose elaborate pattern includes a coloured border, hang alone at the windows but this may represent a summer arrangement. Sadly, the black and white photograph cannot convey the colour scheme. Bonnar prided himself as a colourist and its importance in the firm reflected his father's training with David Ramsay Hay. In spite of the variety of objects the room has a notable repose, so precisely has each object been placed. Refinement, however, has been very much at the expense of mid-Victorian comfort as the token upholstered chair underlines.

42a

42c

Hamilton Palace was the wonder of Scotland; its megalomaniac scale and outstanding contents singlehandedly belied Scotland's conventional image as a place of Calvinist restraint. Because it has been lost it seems particularly important to highlight its important interiors. The ancient Palace had been subject to successive modernisations but assumed its final form from the Tenth Duke of Hamilton, Scotland's premier peer, who believed that he had as sound a claim to the Throne of Scotland as Queen Victoria. The Duke had enormous wealth at his command from coal and minerals and was therefore able to indulge to the full his taste for collecting works of art, and he had agents posted across Europe for this purpose. Although plans for interiors at the Palace were commissioned from leading continental architects including Quarenghi, Percier and Fontaine, the Palace's new front, with its great Corinthian portico supported by monolithic columns, actually arose to the designs of the local Glasgow architect, David Hamilton.

The Duke was careful to preserve much of the historic character of the Palace and his collection was raised on the excellent foundations established by his predecessors. The fame of the Palace's picture collection had long ensured that it was a must for any visitor to Scotland. The new rooms had to be suitably opulent to receive the art treasures which included paintings, tapestries French Royal furniture, entire libraries and quantities of sculpture. The old rooms were redetailed to match. In this task the Duke, as Professor Tait has

described relied heavily on Robert Hume, a London decorator, but he seem also to have been assisted by Scottish workmen including D. R. Hay and Co. The results were undeniably impressive although many visitors were doubtful as to the degree of taste employed. Dr Waagen, Director of the Royal Picture Gallery at Berlin wrote:

As the Duke combined in equal measure a love of art with a love of splendour and was an especial lover of beautiful and rare marbles the whole ameublement was on a scale of costliness with a more numerous display of tables and cabinets of the richest Florentine mosaic than I had seen in any other palace. As a full crimson predominated in the carpets a deep brown in the woods of the furniture, and a black Irish marble, as deep in colour as the nero antico, in the specimens of marble, the general effect was that of the most massive and truly princely splendour; at the same time somewhat gloomy, I might almost say Spanish, in character.

In 1882, thirty years after the Duke Alexander had been laid to rest in his Egyptian sarcophagus beneath the dome of his colossal Mausoleum, the Palace was exposed to the glare of international publicity when the sale of its art treasures was announced, creating a sensation. It was made clear that 'the family portraits and items of a purely family interest' were to be exempted. Surprisingly the only record of the Palace interior

43a

43b

before it was stripped of its stupendous treasures consists of these few photographs by Annan which may have been inspired by the threat of dissolution. The inadequacy of the record is possibly a result of the decision to sell the collection in Christie's London rooms rather than at the Palace in spite of the knowledge that this might detract from ' the material result'. Although the catalogue was photographically illustrated, they show the objects devoid of any context, and the illustrated souvenir catalogue also fails to show the settings. It was perhaps the greatest art sale of the century realising £397,562 and inevitably recalled the Fonthill sale because the Duke had married Beckford's daughter, Susan. Although later photographs [64] show that much of the furniture and all the family portraits remained *in situ* and there was an effort to plug the more obvious gaps, the voluptuous decorations had lost their point. Further indignity was to follow with the exploitation of the coal seams under the Park. The final sale on November 12th, 1919 was to be of the Palace itself and the penultimate lot was one of Duke Alexander's grandest installations:

Lot 570 · The Black Marble Staircase, *with massive balustrade, supported by rectangular banisters carved with acanthus foliage, comprising a double flight of twenty-five steps, and a gallery 40ft wide, the latter supported by bronze figures of Atlas; and three short lengths of similar balustrade to balcony.*

The month permitted for the removal of all lots seems hardly adequate for such a monster. Although the Palace has gone and its role in Scottish architecture has been largely forgotten, its contents comprise the most precious possessions of museums throughout the world and its architecture has been subject to the most spectacular piece of recycling – pieces of it are constantly being rediscovered. In recent years a complete room was discovered in a packing case in America and has been re-erected in Dallas, while the staircase, minus part of a flight awaits assembly in Scotland.

Overleaf: 43e

43c

43d

44: THE ANTIQUE-FILLED ROOMS OF JOHN MARSHALL, 'AN AMATEUR HOUSE DECORATOR' AT 'SOUTHGATE', CRAIGMILLAR PARK, EDINBURGH
1883

In 1882 John Marshall MA, who had begun his career as a barrister at Lincoln's Inn, moved to Edinburgh to take up the prestigious Rectorship of the Royal High School. He acquired a suitably grand house, 'Southgate' in Craigmillar Park, a fashionable villa-quarter but departed from convention by supervising its furnishings himself. Far from being branded an eccentric, the result was such a success that Marshall was invited to give a lecture about the house to the Edinburgh Architectural Association. It was so well received that it was published in 1883 as *Amateur House Decoration* with illustrations 'taken from sketches in the author's house'. As befitted a classicist and a barrister, his account is both stylish, and persuasively argued. It is of great value in charting an individual's changing tastes through the 'domestic auto-biography' which prefaced his discussion of 'Southgate'. This provides a vivid satire on the banalities of conventional taste.

Marshall's first London house had been 'furnished by the "ogre" calling himself the upholsterer' and contained typical horse-hair and mahogany furniture, 'mechanically carved and casually glued', with a centre-table 'neatly bearing in a kind of wheel-spoke pattern, layers of albums and other polite literature'. His independence of spirit began to assert itself with a restless and seemingly aimless shifting about of the pieces, which ended in the ejection of the centre-table. The next stage towards his assumption of personal control over his environment took the form of 'china-mania' and soon the walls of his rooms blossomed out 'in arrays of plates from which the plaster and paper suffered terribly'. As this passion waned, Marshall realised that the experience had heightened his appreciation of colour. The decisive change came through his 'introduction to a really beautiful drawing room, very tiny, but done by an

44b

artist' which was furnished with Persian rugs, Chippendale chairs and Sheraton satinwood. Shortly after this, Marshall moved to Oxford which gave him an 'excuse for a general elimination of all our wretched household goods except some heretofore despised old tables and chairs that had lingered neglected in the attics'. The new rooms were furnished entirely with antiques – his new found 'love' – and this collection was to form the basis of the 'Southgate' interiors when he moved to Edinburgh.

His new home was a typical speculative-builder's villa. Its ugly pretentiousness represented everything Marshall now despised. In the lecture he awards credit to the 'professional decorator' who had assisted him and it seems likely that this was Thomas Bonnar II, who took an active part in the Edinburgh Architectural Association. The Hall has Queen Anne detailing which may have been introduced by Marshall. Instead of the regulation suite of hall chairs and combination lobby-table and hat-stand he substituted a more Picturesque set of Charles II chairs and 'an old inlaid linen chest which may well decorate our hall and accommodate our boots and gloves'. A vignette of the Dining Room shows that

he installed mouldings round the upper walls to recall the low ceilings of his Oxford rooms which he missed. The frieze thus produced prefigures a standard component of late nineteenth-century decoration. The Jacobean buffet must have been an Oxford purchase but the Sheraton sideboard with its tiered superstructure is of standard Scottish type and was probably an Edinburgh purchase. Inevitably, the Dining chairs are Chippendale.

The builder had provided a suitably ambitious Drawing Room on the first floor but in defiance of convention, which must have taken some courage in an Edinburgh headmaster, Marshall rechristened this room the Music Room. To underline its new function a grand piano was emphatically placed in the centre of the room. In place of the regulation and chilly white statuary marble slabs, Marshall installed a fine eighteenth-century carved chimneypiece. A grandfather clock standing in a corner substituted for the regulation mantel-piece clock of temple form. Exemplars which could supply an entire history of eighteenth-century seat furniture took the place of an upholsterer's 'twenty guinea' suite. Mrs Marshall

44a

44c

44e

advertised her services as a portrait painter and she may thus have been responsible for the picture collection which added the final artistic polish to the room. Persian rugs on dark-varnished boards take the place of the fitted Brussels carpet of the early Victorian Drawing Room. Recently two photographs of the Drawing room have been identified in the National Monuments Record of Scotland and they show a much greater degree of detail than the line drawings which then current methods of reproduction required. The photographs reveal Japanese influence in the stencilled frieze and depict the draw-up form of the curtains which discouraged dust and were made of antique damask. They also reveal the Picturesque character of this many layered interior and vividly convey the attraction it must have held for the members of the Edinburgh Architectural Association. No profession was to be more devoted to antique shops than Scottish architects during the late nineteenth century.

44f

This unusually complete survey of the principal rooms at Cullen gives a particularly vivid impression of the over-all look of a Bryce house and the hierarchic way in which different rooms were kitted out. Bryce became Scotland's leading country house architect after his master, William Burn, had moved south to further his career. When the seventh Earl of Seafield inherited Cullen in 1853 it had been half-heartedly classicised and must have seemed unworthy of its dramatic hanging site. With characteristic skill in 1858 Bryce both re-instated and played up the castle's ancient character, while at the same time bringing it up to scratch in terms of the comfort and efficiency expected in a first rate Victorian country house. The photographs show the sweep of public rooms that resulted from some judicious rearrange-

ment and surprisingly minor additions. The interior architecture is unexpectedly modest and the effect derives from the contents.

The decoration is antiquarian in spirit. The long run of family portraits and the more interesting of the inherited furnishings provided a baseline which played up the family's ancient lineage onto which a diverse range of antiques was grafted to ensure that every corner contained something to stimulate the eye. Although the rooms must have been fitted up in 1860, this kind of decoration made it possible to add continuously. It is not known how much Bryce supervised the creation of his interiors. He certainly had a long association with the Edinburgh firm of Bonnar and Carfrae who painted his houses but it seems likely that a specialist decorator

45c

must have helped to assemble the contents. The elements for which Bryce was certainly responsible, such as the design of the plasterwork, seem restrained in comparison to the elaboration of decorative detail in the upholstery, while the chimneypieces seem to be treated more as furnishings than architectural elements.

The series opens with the First Salon [45a] which was an ante room. Its chimneypiece was a fantastic confec-tion of mirror glass and blackamoors designed to show off a panel of naturalistic woodcarving attributed to Grinling Gibbons. Although its pricelessness was stressed in later accounts it actually seems to have been acquired for £14 at a sale in Herefordshire in 1874. The surrounding furniture is appropriately lively to complement this star attraction and yet sober enough for an ante-room. A non-functioning Venetian chandelier, groaning with

45a

45

45b

45c

coloured glass flowers, is practically accompanied by the gas bracket in the form of a coronet, which like the others throughout the suite must have been specially commissioned. The drawing room [45b] has choicer contents surrounding a substructure of comfortable chairs. The curvaceous chimneypiece, one of a pair, must be a further antique import and is much fussier than Bryce's rather perfunctory fretwork plasterwork.

The pair of tapestry carpets, like the modern gilt table and fancy chairs in a Louis XVI mode were probably expensively obtained from Paris, while the cabinets are antique. The curtains are in a sumptuous floral satin in several colours and elaborately detailed. The little centre table is so elaborate that only a carved Baroque dolphin can be picked out with any certainty. The spinning wheel is a Picturesque accessory reflected, like the

5f

45h

45i

45j

statue, in the glass which has also captured the likeness of the photographer himself.

The Picture Room [45c,d] pre-dated Bryce but he may have helped along its old-fashioned character and the chimneypieces were certainly decked with additional carving. The panelling was woodgrained and high-varnished and the ceiling was painted to match. The resplendent curtains with embroidered pelmets and gilded poles are said to date from 1825 and were retained along with the convex girandoles. The curved console tables with their carved superstructures must have been created in 1860. Comfortable chairs are inter-

45g

spersed by yet more spinning wheels and the parrot, which elsewhere might be an exotic centre of attention, takes some time to detect. The Baronial Dining Room [45e,f] was probably conceived around the tapestries. Whereas in the seventeenth century these might have been ruthlessly cut to fit a classical scheme, here Bryce is more likely to have calculated his boldly detailed historicist panelling to eke them out because they had lost their borders. The chimney-piece of inlaid marbles is equally robust. The plate glass windows are framed by the complex lambrequins of the curtains and the character of the room is continued by the seventeenth-century style stuffed chairs with antique painted-leather covers.

By contrast the Boudoir [45g,h] retains its late Georgian interior architecture but it has been overlaid by a very feminine decorative scheme of white moiré wallpaper with deep applied borders which appear to represent larch fronds with fir cones. The same naturalistic pattern is repeated in both the carpet border and the painted porcelain panels which frame the imaginative matching conifer grate. This serves as a background for an impressive display of modern highly enamelled art ceramics which embrace the chandelier and chimney-glass. Sadly only a part of a deeply-buttoned scroll-backed fancy chair is visible. The satin curtains are exaggeratedly full and trail onto the floor. The jardinière contains a cactus and there is yet another spinning wheel. The libraries [45i,j] on the upper floor are appropriately sedate but their Chippendale chairs are the first hint that eighteenth-century British styles are going to supply a further outlet for the collecting instinct. The quilted chair covers look particularly inviting. Because of chances of inheritance these rooms seem to have survived unaltered into the twentieth century.

The late Countess of Seafield devoted much energy to diluting the effect of Bryce's efforts and may have provided some of the inspiration for her relation, Nancy Mitford's first novel *Highland Fling* which is one of the earliest revisionist apologies for The Baronial.

46: THE CASTELLATED AND DOMESTIC INTERIORS OF MACGIBBON AND ROSS
1887–92

If Billings has the honour of producing the most beautiful book ever devoted to Scottish Architecture, David MacGibbon and Thomas Ross share the distinction of having produced the most influential. Their *Castellated and Domestic Architecture of Scotland* appeared in five volumes between 1887 and 1892. Their biographer, Dr David Walker, has shown that this achievement was the more remarkable for having been produced during snatched moments of leisure from their very busy architectural practice. Knowing that they could not compete against Billings' luxurious production methods, MacGibbon and Ross were concerned to produce a much more rounded picture of Scotland's architecture and they placed particular emphasis on plans. Their illustrations were schematic and took advantage of new photographic methods of preparing the plates. They had no illusions as to the merits of their diagrams and wrote in the Introduction:

Our sketches are not intended to imitate or rival the beautiful and artistic etchings of some of our Scottish edifices which have from time to time been published, but simply to represent the Architecture in what appeared to us the most intelligible and effective manner.

In pursuit of providing a full picture, the architects took considerable interest in interiors, but their approach was wholly archaeological as they concentrated on historic detail, editing out any furnishings that obstructed the architecture. Their preparatory and finished drawings are now in the collections of the National Library of Scotland and allow their method to be studied. Ross's rapid pencil sketch survives for one of the rooms in Baillie Macmorran's House in Riddle's Court of the Lawnmarket in Edinburgh. Most unusually, a bureau has been permitted to obtrude and even found its way into the published plate. The finished drawing survives

6a

46b

for one of the rooms in Craig's Close, off the High Street of Edinburgh which demonstrates how Ross worked up the pencil sketches with pen hatching in such a way that it could withstand photographic reduction. Faced by this outstanding Georgian Baroque Bedchamber with its Ionic bed recess, it is revealing that they found the niche over the chimneypiece to be a 'quaint feature'. Only the kettle attests to the fact that the room had fallen in the social scale and was probably an apartment in a near slum. The finished illustration is shown in an actual size reproduction of the Drawing Room at Auchterhouse which unexpectedly has been left with its curtains although the majority of the furnishings have been magicked away with the carpet. Their text reveals the kind of disappointment that all too often awaited the antiquarian following in the wake of an improvers hand:

The house has been so modernised and altered externally that it presents few features of architectural interest. The interior of the drawing-room, however, still retains in the ceiling and mantelpiece a favourable specimen of the style of decoration adopted in the time of the Charleses.

It is impossible to overestimate the influence of these remarkable books which have done so much to inspire succeeding generations of Scottish architects. It is a measure of their impact that William Scott Morton immediately translated their sketch of the thistle frieze at Elcho Castle into his Tynecastle canvas and it thus crops up frequently in turn of the century houses. Although they were far from being the sole culprits, however, it is a fact that the later antiquarians have possibly exerted a disastrous impact on the appreciation of the historic interior. Their ruthless concentration on 'features of architectural interest' and editing away of clutter has all too often been the reality of many restoration schemes and led to a failure to grasp interiors as a unity.

46c

The published catalogues of Wilson's photographic views of Scottish scenery and Picturesque old buildings reflect the scale of the late Victorian mass tourist market. One of the very few interiors listed was this archetype labelled simply 'A Highland Kitchen'. In contrast to Pennant's frisson of distress when faced by the poverty of the Islay weavers cottage in 1772, the motivation behind this photograph seems to be nostalgia, for some of the purchasers it possibly recalled a lost way of life as a result of the great changes during the course of the century separating the two views. The room is in a substantially built house as the impressive chimneylintel indicates, and the dresser with its cut-out heart is well finished and modish. That the occupants are clearly above the poverty line is suggested by the American

clock with its back-painted glass panel. The chair is simple and robust rather than crude while the little children's chairs add to the appealing, sanitised impression. The fireside stool with carrying hand hole, by contrast, is such a basic piece of Scottish furniture that it even appears in the drawing of one of Edinburgh's worst slums [49b]. In the twentieth century the heightened sense of a rural world that was rapidly passing away has led to a number of important initiatives. The Folk Museums at Kingussie and Glamis enable visitors to inspect the domestic artefacts at first hand while the Country Life Archive maintained by the National Museums of Scotland contains extensive photographic records of rural interiors.

48: THE KITCHEN OF THE BURNS' COTTAGE
AT ALLOWAY WHERE THE POET WAS BORN IN 1759
c.1890

Burns Cottage is one of Scotland's longest established tourist attractions and is an important pioneering attempt to furnish an historic interior.

As early as the late eighteenth century when the ownership had passed from the poet's family to the Incorporation of Shoemakers in Ayr, its associations were being exploited commercially as an ale-house. In 1881 the Trustees of the official Burns Monument, nearby succeeded in their bid to acquire the cottage and establish Burns' birthplace as a museum. To this task they brought the same dedication that was expended at Washington's Mount Vernon, in assembling all the available relics of the poet as an early guidebook records:

As soon as they came into occupation, the Trustees earnestly set about making their property a worthy memorial of the Poet, and their energies have been steadily directed to the careful preservation of the original structure, and to the acquisition of genuine

well-authenticated relics of the Poet and his family. An earlier carte-de-visite photograph of *c.*1860 showing the Tam o' Shanter Inn at Ayr (allegedly showing his chair [48b]) provides a vivid testimony to the absurdities of the phoney Burns' memorabilia industry.

It must have been very much more difficult to recover artefacts from this level of society than from that of America's First President and the kitchen is a tribute to the Trustees' ingenuity and honesty:

If we except the fixtures, no article of furniture that formed the original plenishing of the Cottage is now here: without doubt William Burnes took it all with him to his larger holding at Mount Oliphant, and in the subsequent 'flittings' of the family it became outworn or merged in, and indistinguishable from, later acquisitions. In any case there is no reason whatever for asserting that the old furniture exhibited in London in 1918, and claimed to be that which sur-

48a

rounded Burns's birth, was ever the property of his father. The dresser and plate-rack in the kitchen is, almost certainly, coeval with the Cottage itself, as are the curtained bedstance wherein the Poet was born – though its original wooden moveable parts have long since vanished.

If they failed to recover Burn's furniture the Museum is rich in other memorabilia of the poet's lifetime which allows a unique insight into late eighteenth-century Scotland.

8b

49: THE EDINBURGH SLUMS
1891

Although Victorian commercial photographers included many Picturesque views of the exteriors of houses in the Old Town of Edinburgh in their catalogues, there is a notable lack of corresponding interiors. This is because their antiquarian charms concealed some of the worst slums in Britain. That the decline of the former aristocratic lodgings was a gradual one is perhaps suggested by Mrs Stewart Smith's sketch of 1868 [49a] which shows a grand Baroque room which, although it has come down in the world, still seems pleasant enough. Although the city authorities had taken steps to demolish some of the worst slums and replace them by model dwellings there was still plenty of room for private initiatives. These illustrations both come from propagandist tracts. In 1891 the bookseller, James Thin, published a selection of articles written for *The Scotsman* by 'TBM' under the title 'Slum Life in Edinburgh or Scenes in its Darkest Places'. The line drawings are rather less effective than the written description:

49a

The room for which a weekly rent of from one and three pence to half-a-crown is paid is small, dirty and dingy. The walls are black with the smoke and dirt of years; here and there the plaster has fallen off in patches, and reveals the lath beneath. The floor looks as though soap and water were still unknown in these regions; likewise the crazy deal table – if there happens to be one. There may be a chair with a decayed back, but frequently a roughly made stool or an up-turned box does duty instead. And the bed! These lairs – for the word 'bed' may suggest an erroneous idea of luxury – have long been a marvel to us; in as much as it is difficult to imagine how blankets, which presumably were once white, have assumed a hue so dark. They appear to have been steeped in a solution of soot and water – blanket and pillows and mattress, or what stands for such. Generally the bed is a wooden one, a venerable relic of bygone fashions, bought for a trifle from the furniture broker on the other side of the street. But very often a bedstead is not included in the furnishings of the chamber, in which case the family couch consists of a mattress or a bundle of rags, or some straw laid in the least draughty corner of the room, and covered with any kind of rags that can be gathered together.

The photograph is taken from a manuscript entitled 'The Life History of a Slum Child', probably from about the same date but its concluding sections reveal the ameliorating effects of the efforts made by the social and religious reformers whose ranks included Patrick Geddes. Although the photographs are carefully contrived they succeed in their purpose of conveying human misery.

A FAMILY IN A ONE-ROOMED HOUSE.

49b

The Life History of a Slum Child.

This is "a nameless lassie
nursed by her unhappy mother's
unhappier mother in a
room which was not untypical
& which contained.
A chair-bed with old coats for covering
A chair.
A box for a second seat.
A table.
A lamp.
A pot & kettle.
A strip of old worn-out carpet.
A few dishes &odd (indeed odd!)
    ornaments (sic).
And literally Nothing else.
    This was the HOME of the father (who
was in prison when the child was born)
& the Mother who was just 16 years of age.

49c

William Reid inherited control of Morison & Co., a long established and distinguished firm of Edinburgh cabinet-makers and upholsterers, on the death of his father in 1895 but his own career with the firm stretched back to 1873. According to his biographer the success of the business owed much to Reid's personal qualities, as he had been 'endowed with exceptionally fine taste and cultivated the gift diligently'. As a result 'many important clients were attracted to the firm by the reputation of W. R. Reid'. In 1895 he married Margaret Johnston Barton and they occupied apartments above the firm's showrooms at 78 George Street, the capital's premier address for fashionable carriage-trade shops.

Although this fine early New Town house might have suggested a Georgian treatment and furnishing with antiques was an established fashion, these photographs betray a highly sophisticated approach to decoration. At a time when it was becoming fashionable to throw out over-stuffed early Victorian dining chairs and substitute the more elegant discomfort of Chippendale patterns, Reid has selected for his own use a set of Dutch Neo-Classical chairs. The chimney-piece of the same room, however, with its continued marble-framed glass is of a type popularised in Edinburgh by Sir John Robison and admired by J. C. Loudon [21d] which may have been original to the house. Reid's Drawing Room contains a carefully selected collection of antique and modern furniture which share the same elegance of line. It is

50a

50b

interesting that the oval-backed chair, partly hidden by the *bureau plat* is actually from Chippendale's workshop and it is a credit to Reid that he should have picked out an item by this master chair-maker. The same sophistication continues into the bedroom where the modern divan bed with its vase-topped head and foot boards is in a very popular Morison pattern which was supplied in large numbers to the Earl of Iveagh at Elveden Hall in Norfolk, illustrating the range of Reid's commissions. The bedside table appears twice in the photographs and is one of the choicest items in the collection. At some stage it had been liberated from its pair in the State Bedroom at Hopetoun where it had been supplied by James Cullen in 1768.

Reid's many years of training with Morison's equipped him with a special understanding of textiles and their selection has been as fastidious as the furniture. Mrs Reid's family were sanitary engineers and the elegant wash-hand basin in the Dressing Room [50c] shows a marriage of the two families' abilities. Reid's collection of engravings gives the final polish to these rooms. An unusual feature of the way the house was used is that the bedrooms occupied the original first floor Drawing Rooms with the public rooms above. In 1902 Reid retired from the business and transferred the collection to Lauriston Castle, his country villa on the outskirts of Edinburgh. Although he had doubtless purchased the house especially to show off his possessions they were perhaps less in harmony with the rooms designed by William Burn in 1827, than in Neo-Classical George Street. On Mrs Reid's death Lauriston Castle was presented to the City of Edinburgh for preservation as a museum, so Reid's perfect taste can still be appreciated today.

50d

50e

51: THE PHOTOGRAPHIC STUDIO OF MR J.C. BROWN, FALKIRK 1895

The rarity of interior records of ordinary houses is perhaps underlined by the fact that although the camera was always to hand there are hardly any views of photographic studios. This record was taken for a gushing advert of Brown's talents which was inserted in *The Official Guide to the Town Mission Bazaar*. This free publicity was his reward for supplying illustrations for the booklet and the caption relates that 'the most casual observer cannot fail to realise that it obtains to a person of taste'. The ensemble is an exaggerated version of the Picturesque style that prevailed in many contemporary drawing rooms enlivened by basket chairs, palms, exotic textiles and fur. In the distance is a couch that belongs to that peculiar species of furniture unique to photographers' studios and which looks as though it might at any moment dissolve back into the painted backdrop.

52: THE STATION HOTEL AT PERTH PREPARES FOR QUEEN VICTORIA c.1895

Queen Victoria is supposed to have disliked dining on trains and these photographs confirm this. Perth formed the last stage on the Queen's long journey to Balmoral from the South and the Station Hotel was a convenient location for the Royal luncheon. Although the hotel has clearly put its best foot forward and the rooms have been elaborately dressed, draped and decked with flowers a certain grimness, at odds with the plenty of the table, lingers. The rooms, however, reveal a sense of modern fashions through their oriental style carpets, stamped plush upholstery, high-varnished oak dining chairs and a wooden picture rail set at the same height as the windows. Wylie & Lochhead of Glasgow were the furnishing contractors.

51

52a

52b

53a

53b

53c

53d

53e

53f

53: 'A NORTHERN HOME', ARTHUR SANDERSON'S HOUSE AT 25 LEARMONTH TERRACE, EDINBURGH 1897

William Scott Morton (1840–1903) was an inventive genius who, after an initial training in architecture, followed by a spell on the fringe of Fine Art, applied his considerable powers to decoration in all its many branches. With a passionate faith in the Scottish workman and in spite of his own success in London, he set up business in the Tynecastle district of Edinburgh which gave its name to the works. The range of his inventions is extraordinary and his patents embraced a cast iron grate with an integral coal scuttle. He is best remembered for the embossed canvas imitating stamped leather which could be fashioned into anything from Adam ceiling kits to picture frames. Tynecastle canvas was exported throughout the world.

The greatest tribute to his abilities was paid by Arthur Sanderson, whose fortune derived, from the spirit trade, when he asked the designer to assume overall responsibility for his new house at 25 Learmonth Terrace. This was created for the display of Sanderson's outstanding art collection which had much in common with the great collections founded by American millionaires in that it embraced old master and British pictures, antique furniture and oriental porcelains. If the outside of the house was severe and conventional, the inside was so richly decorated that, with its glittering contents, it must have created the effect of an astonishing treasure chest that had few parallels in Scotland. This important commission stimulated Scott Morton to further invention, including the idea of inlaying the canvas panels with glass tesserae, but it seems to have been Sanderson himself who suggested the ultimate challenge for the Tynecastle canvas – imitating the Parthenon frieze. Needless to say, Scott Morton soon had his restored copy in production and the frieze joined the list of the firm's exports but Sanderson reserved the right to it in the County of Midlothian as the advertising pamphlet confirms.

The rooms were in a kaleidoscopic range of styles, partly reflecting the contents but also the styles deemed appropriate by the late nineteenth century for their different functions. The decorations embraced the entire history of art and began in the Hall with stained glass by Cottier depicting an incident in the story of Theseus.

The Dining room was 'British', with pictures by Reynolds, Gainsborough and Turner, and antique furniture in the Chippendale and Sheraton styles. The Parthenon frieze provided the key to the staircase and led through a door studded with enamels, to the Adamesque Drawing Room with its alabaster chimneypiece, a brass grate inlaid with Wedgwood and choice satinwood furniture whose decorative painting, inevitably, was attributed to Angelica Kauffmann. The Billiard Room was the most substantial interior with its two floor levels and richly carved screen. One of the bedrooms was in the Louis XIII style but with all the conveniences of modern plumbing. There can scarcely have been a corner without an art treasure but the photographs also reveal a very skilled hand behind the arrangement of each item which is particularly noticeable in the groupings of porcelain on every projection. Although these photographs which are reproduced from the *Art Journal* of 1897 are not of the best quality they are able to recapture the rarified atmosphere of this house which also unexpectedly demonstrated its country of origin as Cosmo Monkhouse wrote in the accompanying text:

It is worthy of note that the whole of its elaborate and beautiful decoration has been designed by a Scotsman, and that most, if not all, of the work has been executed in Scotland. From the Albert Works in Edinburgh issued all the fine woodcarving and I know not what else. In Scotland was invented the Tynecastle canvas, employed, as we have seen, almost throughout the house for wall coverings, ceilings, panellings, reliefs, and other purposes; most of the carpets were woven in Glasgow and a great many other things, too numerous to mention were fashioned north of the Tweed. There are many other signs that Mr Sanderson, in creating this 'lordly pleasure-house', has thought not only of himself or of Art, but also of his country.

Although the contents are now dispersed, with the pictures having ended up *en bloc* in Eastern Europe, the interiors have been preserved in excellent condition by the Auxiliary Air Force.

54: THE LORIMERS RESTORE KELLIE CASTLE
c.1897

Kellie Castle, a rambling tower house in Fife with fine decorative plasterwork, had fallen into decay when it was rescued in 1878 by Professor James Lorimer of Edinburgh University. He was unable to purchase outright and could only obtain a lease. For this reason, coupled with its use as a holiday home, his restoration was unusually conservative. The view of the Dining Room comes from a set of photographs by Milliken of Kirkcaldy which belonged to the architects Tarbolton and Ochterlony. The photographer's purpose was primarily antiquarian and the rest of the set consists only of plasterwork details of Balcaskie. Perhaps unwittingly, therefore, in this view of the painted panelling and heraldic ceiling he has captured something of the quality of the Professor's taste. The narrow, and thus, presumably, inexpensive panel of tapestry is the only traditional antiquarian element in his furnishings and he has retained the simple late eighteenth-century chimney-piece which in his account of the Castle's history is described as being Queen Anne. In his choice of Chippendale chairs he was following recent fashions but

the use of two different patterns was unusually relaxed. It is the simple rag rug made up from strips that provides the strongest evidence of the operation of a sophisticated taste. Professor Lorimer was working in the Scottish idiom of the same international folk revival that also inspired Carl Larsson in Sweden

Their childhood at Kellie was to be a formative influence on the subsequent careers of his sons John, the artist, and Robert, the architect. After their father's death in 1890, John inherited the lease and in 1897 the brothers improved the Drawing Room by reinstating its Baroque panelling which had been concealed in part by wallpaper. In her study of the castle's restoration Harriet Richardson has contrasted the father's tolerant conservatism and enthusiasm for earlier phases of the castle's history, with his sons' greater feeling for the later Baroque decorations. They played up their more formal character, self-consciously working in the idiom of an historical style with the rather pretentious monogrammed cartouches and commissioning a stylish over-mantle painting from the artist, Phoebe Traquair.

Facing: 54a   54b

Sir William Fraser (1816–1898) was the doyen of Scottish genealogists. Although trained as a lawyer, he entered the public service and became Deputy Keeper of Records for Scotland. He is remembered, however, for the long series of family histories produced in his spare time 'at the expense of the historic families whose fortunes they chronicled' and whose style has been described as 'dry as dustish'. Sir William made no structural changes to his New Town property and his study must have been intended as the Dining Room with its black chimneypiece and pilaster marking the sideboard end. The paintwork could date from the 1820s with its standard Dining Room scheme of plain painted walls, oak grained panelling and mahogany grained door whose copal varnish has been burnished to a glassily reflective surface. With typical antiquarian taste, Sir William has selected a Carolean armchair for himself and the impress of his back remains upon its velvet upholstery from his long labours. Two of his fat family chronicles with their distinctive gilt on scarlet coronetted bindings lie on the table.

Interestingly the damask table cover with its snowflake pattern matches the carpet although most of the latter has been covered by a drugget to protect it. Portraits of great Scots and modern friends and collaborators look down upon his labours. The distinctive feature of the room is the impressive array of ancient oak with genuine Scottish chairs partnered by a more dubious

55a

buffet and oak carvings. Sir William's researches among family muniments must have given him valuable opportunities to add to this collection but since the taste for early oak was so well established among the Edinburgh lawyers of his generation, these prizes could have been as easily assembled from the auction rooms of nearby George Street.

This photograph comes from an album recording the collection before its dispersal by Dowells of Edinburgh in 1898. Among several philanthropic legacies, Sir William left £25,000 for housing the Edinburgh poor. His study makes an interesting comparison with that of another bachelor, John Miller Gray, which was recorded as the frontispiece to a memorial volume of his writings. Gray (1850–1894) was a much younger man and far from rich, but his study at 28 Gayfield Square also occupied a New Town Dining Room. His family had lost their savings in a bank failure during Gray's childhood and so he was denied a University education. Gray entered the

Bank of Scotland but devoted his spare time, to belles-lettres and art criticism which enabled him to compete successfully for the post as first curator of the newly established Scottish National Portrait Gallery in 1884. He died prematurely, but he had been able to set the new institution on a firm footing. His study reflects his aesthetic tastes with its notes of both Chinamania and, Japanoiserie in the woodcuts, while at least some of his chairs might have gained Morris's approval. The crazy extension to the gas light is its most arresting feature. Writing to a friend about a previous house he recorded that:

While I was away my room has been getting painted … I have not been able to call the colour-scheme of my room by any such fine name as Whistler adopts for his 'arrangement', it is not a 'Nocturne in blue and silver' or anything of that sort. I have shortly titled it An Afternoon in Brown and Yellow with an occasional moment in Green.

55b

Kinnaird Castle is a very large, chateau-style country house of 1854, by David Bryce. These photographs come from an album of 1898 which is unusual not only because the interiors are shown with their carefully posed occupants, but because of its foray through the green baize door to record the highly efficient kitchen commensurate with the scale of the establishment and presided over by the rather grim cook, as well as the laundry and laundrymaid.

56a

56b

57: PROFESSOR GEORGE BALDWIN BROWN
AT HOME IN THE NEW TOWN OF EDINBURGH
c.1900

For fifty years from 1880 until his resignation in 1930, Professor George Baldwin Brown was the Watson Gordon Professor of Fine Art at Edinburgh University. During this long period he occupied a number of addresses in George Square and the West End of Edinburgh. He was an enthusiastic photographer and his surviving negatives include views of more than one of his homes. In this selection, which may be a conflation, the decoration of the New Town house is up to date. The newly decorated Drawing Room is exemplary with its quietly patterned paper, toning cornice, flat painted woodwork and unfitted carpets. The furniture, however, with the exception of the light modish Hepplewhite revival shield-back chair, is old fashioned and much of it must have been inherited, which seems the kindest explanation for the upright piano.

Brown's early interest in art was stimulated by his sculptor uncle, H. S. Leifchild and the cabinet deco-

rated with carved figures and the centre table have the air of studio props. The plentiful ornaments, ceramics and textiles reflect the breadth of the Professor's interests and travels. The staircase is equally fashionably papered with a varnished dado. The seventeenth-century style chair is upholstered in the hide of an exotic beast. The Professor's study-dressing room has a jaunty paper, strewn with daisies. His camera lies ready for use on the table and a later negative of the same view shows the walls covered in pictures and additional bookshelves. The most memorable photograph is the view of the marbled chimneypiece where, in order to accommodate the bric-à-brac, an additional chimneyshelf has been resorted to. A photograph of Gainsborough's The Hon. Mrs Graham in the collection of the National Gallery incongruously rubs her shoulders with tins of photographic toner, orientalia and a pair of animal skulls.

57a

57b

NO SMOKING ALLOWED.

57f

This photograph demonstrates the technical advances that made it possible for even an unskilled amateur to take snapshots by the end of the nineteenth century. It comes from a smart morocco album, bound in Bond Street, which bore 'Balmacaan' in large gilt letters on its cover and belonged to the Countess of Craven. On the flyleaf she has proudly written 'These photographs were all taken with my little Kodak, Cornelia Craven'. Although a far from competent photographer, her enthusiasm for recording her Scottish home may reflect her transatlantic background because she was the only daughter of Bradley Martin of New York. The urbanity of her rooms with a Reynolds and the Louis XVI style furniture (probably a temporary installation in this rented property) are a reminder of the very international character of the Highlands whose shooting lodges can contain the strangest things. One of the most startling ensembles must have been Lord Tweedmouth's collection of early Wedgwood and English eighteenth-century porcelains installed in Adamesque rooms by Wright and Mansfield at Guisachan in Inverness-shire.

59: LADY HENRIETTA GILMOUR
RECORDS HER DRAWING ROOM AT MONTRAVE
c.1900

These photographs of Montrave were taken in about 1900 by Lady Henrietta Gilmour who was a very much more dedicated amateur photographer than the Countess of Craven. The negatives were retrieved from their specially made slots in her fully equipped photographic studio at Montrave by Kitty Cruft of the National Monuments Record of Scotland shortly before the house was demolished. They reveal Lady Henrietta's eye for composition which was closely akin to the method by which these densely furnished rooms were constructed. The elaborate drapery across the arch and the other features of the rooms show the new enthusiasm for textiles that was a characteristic of the 1890s. The variety of luxurious fabrics in this single interior is extraordinary and includes cut velvet, damask and silk lampas in several colours of thread. They are used with a freedom that would have amazed the eighteenth century although almost all the patterns take their inspiration from this period. This profligacy may reflect their relatively low cost as a result of industrialisation. All of the traditional patterns have been altered to suit wider nineteenth-century looms. One of the tables which has been especially made to receive the many palms is entirely fabricated from textiles. The overall composition is enlivened by the individual arrangements on every surface in an extension of the Picturesque system which has been heightened to the extent that it makes even Cullen [45] look underfurnished. These rooms also reveal the new importance of the upholsterer who profited from this short-lived fashion.

59b

60: THE MATHER FAMILY
AT 16 LEAMINGTON TERRACE, EDINBURGH
1900

During the late nineteenth century improvements in both cameras and film made photography a much less troublesome hobby for amateurs. Remarkably few people bothered to record their own houses, however, and this survey from a family photograph album is one of the most complete yet discovered. Number 16 Leamington Terrace was the home of Alexander Mather and was conveniently situated within easy walking distance of 'Alexander Mather and Son, Millwrights, Engineers and Ironfounders' at Fountainbridge. Here, he and his wife brought up their family of five daughters and a son. Their principal interest was music and the children performed as a sextet, as their album shows. It is not clear which member of the family was the photographer, but the ranks of photographs on the Drawing Room walls suggest that it may have been a serious pursuit. The survey is of particular interest because the Mathers do not seem to have been very concerned about decoration and the photographs seem to be informal. Their home must have been typical of thousands of others. The effect is of many layers of taste and furniture superimposed. The ormolu mounted cabinet in the Drawing Room and the parents' half-tester bedstead may have been inherited but the vaguely Queen Anne chiffonier with its *en suite* chairs may have been bought on their marriage. Chinamania and Japanoiserie have also left their mark. Some of the more modish details may repre-

sent the input of the growing children, but the effect is far from smart or up-to-date.

The Hall [60a] has the standard Minton encaustic tiles in the 'harmonious' colours which excited the Victorians but which seem so drab to today's taste. The walls are stencilled with a large-scale pattern and there is the standard combination hat, coat and umbrella stand. A rope mat is placed on the front step. The Staircase Hall has a riot of patterns in the varnished dado paper, floral wall-face and carpet. The stone stairs [60b] have been painted white and the statuary of Flora and the girl and puppy may date from an earlier decorative scheme. The furry mats at the doorways and the portière to the Drawing Room door not only look cosy but must have effectively prevented draughts. There are views of each corner of the Drawing Room [60d–g] which is set for afternoon tea – perhaps it was Mrs Mather's 'At Home' day. The folding tiered cake stand was a common, but now vanished, piece of furniture relating to this ceremony. There are potted plants in the bay window and the clutter is far from being as exaggerated as the very 'decorated' effects, of houses like Montrave. The Dining Room [60h–j] is set for a more substantial tea and characteristically is much darker in tone than the Drawing Room above. With a high-varnished patterned dado-paper, it also has an array of oil-paintings in substantial gold frames unlike the small-scale works in the Drawing

60a

60b

60c

60d

60e

60f

60g

60h

60i

60j

60k

60l

60n

60m

Room. The particularly elaborate flowers on the dinner table may survive from a party although flowers were a prerequisite of every late-Victorian Dining Room. The practical wall-press has had its door removed to turn it into a Chinamania display area. The black chimney-piece and Turkey patterned rug are survivors from much longer established fashions. There seems to have been a bedroom on the ground floor [60k], but the two others which were recorded, seem to be the children's rooms in the attics [60l,m]. One has an imaginatively-used frieze paper while another has a hygienic and practical painted iron-bedstead on which the family pet is, unhygienically, lolling. The most unusual photograph of the series is that of the Kitchen [60n] with a view through to the scullery beyond. It has stout shelves, a practical dresser and wooden-seated chairs. The woman's smart overall and high-heels suggests that she is Mrs Mather rather than the maid.

Such were the dictates of propriety that the Victorian photographer needed an exceedingly good reason to gain admittance to the bedroom quarters. The most exceptional of these three photographs is also the earliest and shows the Psyche Bedroom at Crawford Priory which takes its name from the subject of the cycle of French wallpaper. This was sufficiently unusual to merit inclusion in a survey of this house which was otherwise confined to the public rooms and the Chapel. The wallpaper was probably installed by Thomas Bonnar I, the Edinburgh decorator and most famous pupil of D. R. Hay. Bonnar had worked extensively for the Earl of Glasgow, who is principally remembered as a benefactor of the Episcopal Church. After Bonnar's death in 1873

the Earl remarked of Bonnar's Chapel that 'It remains a monument to Mr Bonnar's good taste and excellent judgment'. The room predated the installation of the paper and Bonnar has ingeniously introduced the stencilled fictive panelling whose style complements the subject matter, so that the small scale of the paper panels is satisfactorily related to the tall proportions of the room. The handsome suite of furniture is reputed to be by Whytock of Edinburgh. Sadly, in their published catalogue of charges, Whytock made a point of not publishing illustrations of their designs, to prevent espionage by their competitors. The room is unified by the use of the same brocade whose geometric pattern, like that of the carpet, shows the successful influence of the

61a

design reformers and the room is thus a good example of the very best taste of Edinburgh's premier firms. Although D. R. Hay had argued vehemently that wallpaper was unsuited to the damp climate of Scotland, the Scots proved enthusiastic purchasers of the most elaborate papers including French panorama cycles, but very little survives today.

The other two rooms attracted their photographers' attention on account of the fame of their alleged occupants but in each case their interest today arises as much from their also providing a record of prosaic, and once typical, aspects of nineteenth-century bedrooms. Cawdor Castle was Shakespeare's contribution to Scottish tourism. The fanciful murals of 'King Duncan's Room' [61b] which one account identifies as being in 'charcoal' were perhaps introduced in an attempt to overcome the tourists' disappointment that the modern castle retained so few vestiges of this most interesting but remote early period. The deerskin rug, the ancient armchair and the primitive fire of logs are also attempts to impart more character to a room which otherwise is a perfectly ordinary specimen of the standard of comfort that was provided in a country house bedroom in the second quarter of the nineteenth century. The four-post

bedstead is upholstered in a starched chintz and its construction is so simple that it could have been homemade. It has a typical white Marseilles bedcover woven to look like stitched quilting. The floor is covered in a cosy looking flatwoven Scotch carpet which bears two medallions, side by side, in each width. A subsequent photograph of the room shows bare boards, doubtless in pursuit of an enhanced antiquarian effect.

The photograph of Prince Charles' Room [61c] at Culloden House is taken from the sale catalogue of 1897 when the contents of this elegant Neo-Classical house of c.1780 were dispersed. It thus considerably post-dated the battle which was the tragic reason for the Prince's supposed visit. Such was the power of the myth, however, that the furnishings of the room, like that at Cawdor, resisted fashionable changes. The photograph provides an exceedingly rare illustration of the kind of pretty wallpaper with its stripes and flowers that was deemed suitable for a bedroom c.1800. Equally rare is the carpet with its small-scale pattern, which the catalogue describes as a 'Scotch' and which is fitted to the room. It seems to have an *en suite* pile hearthrug. The chintz upholstery of the bedstead may also be a survival from the same initial campaign of fitting up the room.

61b

61c

62: SIR ROWAND ANDERSON'S OWN HOUSE, 'ALLERMUIR' AT 15 WOODHALL ROAD, EDINBURGH
c.1900

When these photographs were taken Sir Rowand Anderson was firmly established as the undisputed head of the architectural profession in Scotland. Although these rooms have been overlaid like a jackdaw's nest by a glittering array of choice objects which reflect the wide range of the architect's interests, the essential character of the original villa, which he had designed for himself in 1879, has remained unchanged. 'Allermuir' was regarded as a highly innovatory design, as Sam McKinstry has pointed out, because although it was unquestionably in a Scottish idiom with its crow-stepped gable on the garden front it represented a distillation of the national style cleansed of the decorative fripperies like pepperpot turrets which had so attracted earlier exponents of

the Picturesque version of the Baronial. Although the interior panelling recalls historical periods, the detailing of the rooms is as austere as the exterior, with the plainest of drawing room chimneypieces. The effect of strength and enclosure implied by the Dining Room beams and the deep arch of the Drawing Room bay is notable and contrasts with the flimsy, overly-ornamented character of the standard speculative villa of the day. Some of the original contents can easily be spotted, such as the pair of stamped plush upholstered oak chairs in the Drawing Room, but the rooms have swelled with the spoils of many years of discriminating antique collecting. Anderson belonged to the generation that was most deeply affected by Chinamania and the

62a

· 143 ·

rooms were planned to display the beginnings of his very serious collection of oriental porcelain in glazed cabinets and niches. Anderson unlike the younger generation of architects does not seem to have developed an equivalent interest in furniture which is as practical and modern as his player-piano, although there are two Dutch buffet chests of drawers. In spite of the architectural austerity, the rooms betray a more sophisticated taste through the Venetian chandeliers and the many bevel-plated glasses over the chimney.

Anderson's taste must have developed through his contact with the Marquess of Bute for whom he designed Mount Stuart. In addition he maintained a holiday home in Tangiers which doubtless explains the presence of the 'Cairene' table. The modern dining chairs reflect Anderson's attempts to instill a Scottish idiom of design into a developing generation of Scottish architects and craftsmen through the curriculum of his inspiring Edinburgh School of Applied Art which he both founded and directed. Measured drawings of Scotland's historic architecture and craftsmanship were central to the School's activities [62d] and these informed scholarly reproductions are typical of the taste which resulted. Sadly Sir Rowand Anderson's only daughter had died in childhood and the aged architect gave much thought to the disposal of his collections. He presented the best of the porcelain to Holyrood, the finest plate and tableware went to his beloved Royal Company of Archers, while much useful household furniture was left, along with a town house at 15 Rutland Square, to the Royal Incorporation of Architects in Scotland, which he had refounded.

62b

TWO CHAIRS FROM HOLYROOD PALACE EDINBURGH
THE PROPERTY OF THE LATE DUKE OF HAMILTON &c
COVERED WITH GREEN SILK
INCH SCALE PLAN OF CARVED CHAIR
INCH SCALE PLAN OF LEATHER CHAIR
COVERED WITH LEATHER

62d

62c

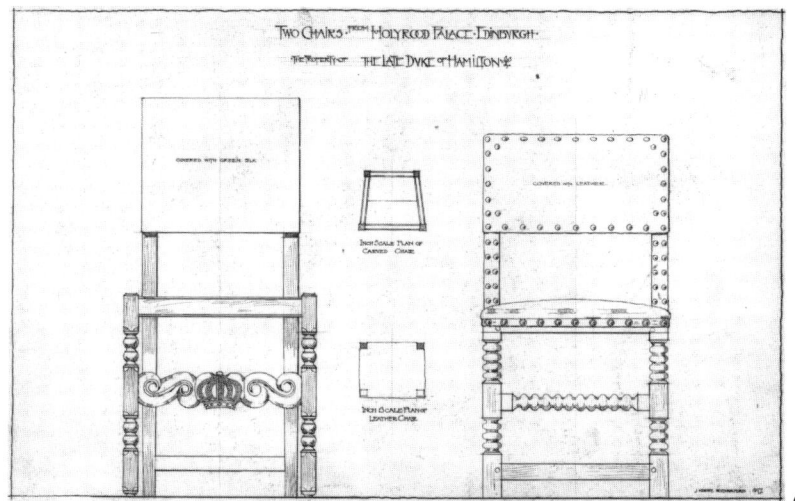

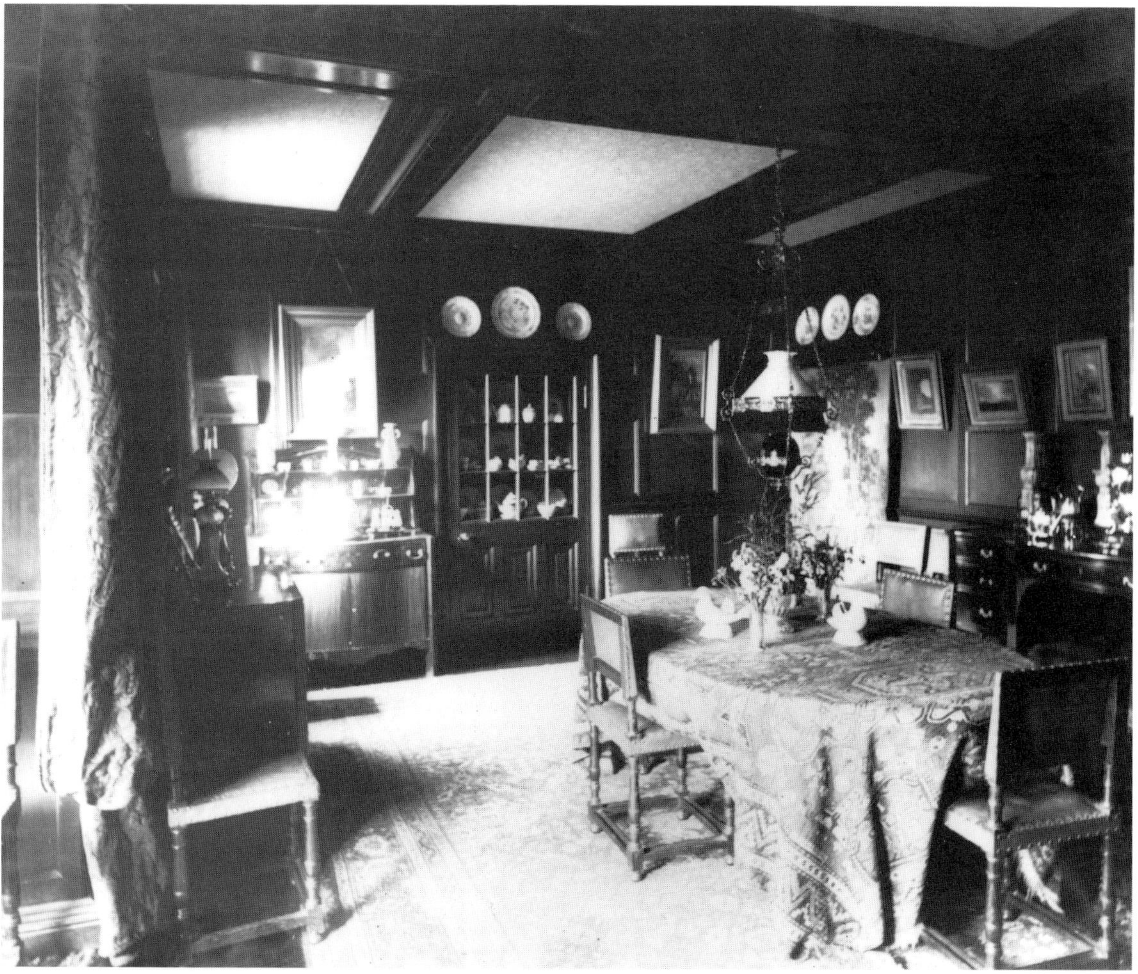

The idea of bringing new life back to a ruined Scottish castle has proved such a potent force that there is hardly a single roofless tower house left. Varying degrees of taste have been brought to the exercise but it is generally agreed that when, in 1892, Robert Lorimer was commissioned by R. W. R. Mackenzie, a wealthy collector, to restore Earlshall, the twenty-eight-year-old architect acquitted himself with perfect tact. He was fortunate to have an especially beautiful subject to work on and his success reflects his formative years spent at Kellie Castle, nearby. Earslhall made Lorimer's name, and it became well-known through publication by *Country Life*. These photographs, however, by an unknown photographer, seem to evoke its romantic spirit rather more successfully than the brightly lit magazine photographs which play up the architecture rather than the collections. By the 1890s, and building on Billings' pioneer efforts, there was both a deeper understanding of earlier decoration and a greater willingness to compromise and dispense with modern comforts in the face of original archaeological detail. This is exemplified in Lorimer's careful restoration of the original painted decoration of the Gallery's barrel vaulted boarded ceiling which had been grievously damaged. Although D. R. Hay had been interested during the 1840s in surviving examples of this robust school of Scottish decoration there had been little attempt to revive them until antiquarians like Lyons began to record and publish examples in the archaeological journals. In the Hall, all the furniture is antique and there has been a great effort to dress the Buffet with pewter, in a self-conscious revival of a once popular Scottish feature. There has been no attempt to interfere with the natural state of the furs.

During the 1890s textiles came to play a major role in the interior and here they are all antique, such as the tapestry panels and fragments. Antique needlework has been used for upholstery and the embroidered top card table is characteristic of Mackenzie's taste. With its topiary gardens, Earlshall was an idyll of old world fashions.

63a

63b

63c

Although photographers' interference with furniture arrangements has been remarked upon in preceding commentaries, these photographs have been included as a reminder of a more serious impediment to photographic records. High standards of housekeeping to prolong the life of costly furnishings ensured that the great state rooms of country houses spent most of their lives muffled under protective coverings. The photograph of Drumlanrig [64a] comes from a large collection of photographs taken by the architect Henry Kerr on outings by the Edinburgh Architectural Association. Although this was a prestigious society, they apparently did not merit the full undressing of the Drawing Room and so the carpet remained rolled up and the chandeliers were concealed in their bags.

The view of Hamilton Palace [64b] records an even rarer practice and shows an only half-hearted removal of the case covers from the central line of furniture whilst the perimeter chairs remain in their dust wraps, as do the pelmets. The curtains themselves have been placed in store and, perhaps most labour intensive of all the entire carpet whose design reflected the ceiling com-

partments, has been covered in a white damask drugget the diamond pattern of which can just be discerned. The revelation of the carpet thus entailed moving every item of furniture in the room.

64a

64b

65: BEDFORD LEMERE'S PHOTOGRAPHS OF CHARLES RENNIE MACKINTOSH'S HILL HOUSE AT HELENSBURGH 1904

The technical ability to publish photographic plates at commercially viable rates was to have far-reaching effects for architects and designers. Whereas previously, the photographic records had had to be converted into line illustrations [44], the quality of the original photograph now became all important. Through his considerable skills, the photographer Bedford Lemere became indispensable to the leading architects of the day. Even Scottish architects found it was well worth his travelling expenses from London in order to have their works flattered. In addition to publicity through publication, photographs were now deemed permissible for entry to architectural exhibitions. Many architects also maintained photograph albums which were useful in discussions with clients whose original introduction to the architect was now as likely to have come from a published or exhibited photograph as from a first hand encounter with one of his buildings. In 1904 the photographer was fortunate to have as his subject the Hill House, the Helensburgh villa which Charles Rennie Mackintosh had newly-designed for the publisher,

Walter H. Blackie. This is work of striking originality and beauty, and the impact of the interiors is greatly promoted by the photographer's ability to enliven them using the play of light. These views are printed from the original glass negatives and even the intricate subtleties of the stencilling has been captured. In his authoritative study of Mackintosh's furniture designs, Roger Billcliffe has shown that these photographs must have been taken before such essential features as the Drawing Room furniture had been completed and a fashionable antique Chippendale chair has been pressed into service. Interestingly, although the house was occupied, there seems to be a deliberate attempt to create a lived-in look through the lit fire, the apparently casually placed books and hassock and the card plate on the table in the Staircase Hall. As in so many photographs of Victorian drawing rooms in this book the Hill House has been carefully dressed with flowers for the photographer's visit.

Overleaf: 65c

65a

65b

The Hill House provides a stimulating contrast with the nearby Long Croft which was designed at the same time by A. N. Paterson, the Glasgow architect, for his own family. Both take their inspiration from Scotland's historic architecture but their expression is very different. Paterson's initial ambition was to be an artist but his family argued that since they were already supporting his brother, James, in this hazardous profession, the younger boy's artistic interests must find a more practical outlet in architecture. On the advice of Sir John Burnet, Paterson studied in Paris, which gives his work a certain urbanity.

The Long Croft employs the Baronial style but it is characteristic of Paterson's approach to architecture that it is employed in a very sculptural way and that the house bears numerous artistic embellishments including figurative sculpture and decorative painting. The house was intended to supply a setting for Paterson's collections which followed very much in the spirit of

Marshall's *Amateur House Decoration* [44] but here there was no compromise with commerce because the house was at one with its contents. The Long Croft was therefore a representative example of the 'House Beautiful' and the perfection of these small British villas was much admired by the German critic, Hermann Muthesius, during his visit to Britain. At the Long Croft, however, art was created as well as worshipped, because not only did Paterson have a studio there, but his wife Margaret Hamilton was a painter and embroideress who found inspiration in the flowers which filled the garden and were liberally displayed throughout the rooms.

These photographs were probably taken by the artist, James Paterson, on one of his visits. Although technically imperfect, they convey the atmosphere of the house shortly after it was built and provide an unusually intimate insight into family life. Maggie Paterson has been carefully composed at her embroidery frame in the Drawing Room bow, appropriately placed beneath the

66a

Guthrie and Wells stained glass panel dedicated to embroidery. The furnishings are a mixture of antiques and modern pieces in traditional styles. Mary Viola is practising the piano beneath a Baroque embroidered altar-frontal which has been incorporated into the Drawing Room's decorations. In the Dining Room, the chairs are Chippendale and the table is decorated with chrysanthemums. Helensburgh played an important part in A. N. Paterson's architectural practice and his studio at the Long Croft had an independent access for tradesmen. He is photographed at his drawing board and although he had designed the desk himself, it is typical that he should have selected an eighteenth-century chair for his professional labours. Paterson was a particularly original designer of chimney-pieces and the one in the studio is said to have been ornamented by George Walton.

66c

66d

66b

67: SIR ROBERT LORIMER'S
OWN DINING ROOM AT 54 MELVILLE STREET, EDINBURGH
c.1910

Although Lorimer was attracted by the social advantages of a residential address in the West End of Edinburgh's New Town, nothing could have been more unfashionable than the understated Greek Revival interiors of late-Georgian Melville Street. His refitting of the Dining Room was conceived around a fine Gothic tapestry which had been rejected by clients after it had been sent over on approval from Paris – much to Lorimer's glee, as Peter Savage has described in his study of the architect. Lorimer's interest in Gothic art had been stimulated through his friendship with Sir William Burrell. An appropriately medieval setting was created with a panelled ceiling incorporating carved bosses, applied panelling on the walls, an oriel window whose leaded lights held stained glass, and a chimney-piece which bore metal dishes like a buffet and the date '1903'. Lorimer liked to burn wood rather than coal and the narrow fireplace was surrounded by enchanting tin-glazed tiles

depicting colourful birds. The carpetless floors were relaid with wide oak boards which rather extravagantly run the length of both rooms. It must have been Lorimer's idea to introduce the double doors to provide a dramatic approach to the new room because all New Town Dining-Rooms had an unbroken side-board wall opposite the windows. The furniture is a mixture of antiques and modern pieces, like the extending dining table, which he designed in the spirit of earlier styles. Lorimer was equally adept at metalwork design and his lightfittings accept the possibilities of the new electric light and were made by Henshaws of Edinburgh. The room was painted dark green with gilt ceiling bosses. The effect is anything but cheerful and his family's nickname of the 'funeral parlour' seems well deserved. From 1966 until 1983 this room was the hub of the National Monuments Record of Scotland whose largest collection comprises Lorimer's office drawings.

68: PATRICK ADAM PAINTS F. T. TENNANT'S
LORIMER DRAWING ROOM AT HYNDFORD, NORTH BERWICK
c.1910

Although many Scottish artists have occasionally produced views of interiors, Patrick Adam seems to have been the only painter to specialise in this genre. Adam had settled in East Lothian which was a popular situation because of its proximity to both Edinburgh and excellent golf courses. The owners of the architect-designed villas in the area soon became Adam's patrons. Sir Patrick Ford's patronage embraced an illustrated biographical study entitled *Interior Paintings by Patrick W Adam RSA* published in 1920. Because it is illustrated in colour it thus supplies an important element to contemporary interiors which is necessarily lacking in black and white photographs. His painting of Hyndford, North Berwick, is important as a colour record of a Lorimer room because hardly any survive with paintwork, furniture and textiles intact.

The room had been added to F. T. Tennant's house in 1903 to serve as a spacious Drawing Room. It shows the taste for panelling which Lorimer promoted but here it is in the French style which the architect favoured for the drawing rooms of wealthy clients. The woodwork was executed by Scott Morton and Co. who became indispensable to Lorimer and many other architects of the period for the carving – as well as the detailing – of their architectural woodwork. The asymmetry of the door, although copied from French rococo precedents, betrays the whimsical strand in Lorimer's artistic personality. The cult of the white drawing room was an aesthetic taste. Lorimer had a similar drawing room in his Edinburgh House and wrote movingly of the pleasure it gave him. The room is furnished with antiques in a very watered down version of contemporary Picturesque taste. Although Adam has relished the rich patterns of the screen, piano cover and upholstery, the room is notably free of soft furnishings and the bareness of the wide carpetless oak boards is typical of Lorimer's personal preferences. His curtains were always very simple in character. The screen just reveals a revived Buffet niche for the display of china which is a reformed altar to Chinamania. The success of Lorimer's rooms was the result of skilful editing of many contemporary trends. In Glasgow, Charles Rennie Mackintosh gave a very different expression to the white drawing room.

69: BONNAR AND COMPANY'S
SHOWROOM AT 58 GEORGE STREET EDINBURGH
c. 1910

This unusual photograph of a decorator's Saloon comes from an album of photographs by Alexander Hutchison who was an Edinburgh joiner and amateur photographer. Many of the photographs of interiors may therefore show houses in which his firm had worked. This view probably shows Bonnar's showroom which was then established at 58 George Street. The most arresting feature is the phalanx of sample boards showing marbling and graining with imitation inlays which by the time the photograph was taken were of historic interest rather than of any practical use although they usefully displayed the firm's lineage. The doors may come from the firm's installations at the 1851 and 1862 Exhibitions

and like the ceiling show the firm's fondness for cherubs. The walls are decorated with a variant on Hay's gold stencilling. The oil painting may be by David Scott whose reputation had been championed by the firm's founder, Thomas Bonnar I. The accent on art rather than commerce may be a reminiscence of Hay's Saloon at 90 George Street which was the finest private picture gallery in Edinburgh and included works by Turner and the artists of the emergent Scottish school. Hay was a close personal friend of both David Roberts and Robert Scott Lauder. The Thonet chairs show that the Saloon was for the carriage-trade, enabling customers to select their patterns and colours in a leisurely fashion.

70a

· 156 ·

The country house articles published each week by *Country Life* founded by Edward Hudson in 1897 comprise a major source for records of Scottish interiors. The relatively generous coverage devoted to Scotland reflects this country's important place in the shooting and golfing activities of many of its readers. Although there was, perhaps understandably, an early preference for castles, the wide interests of its editor ensured that the magazine also played an important part in furthering the career of Sir Robert Lorimer through publicising, his works.

The article on Pollok by Lawrence Weaver records the completion of a campaign of improvement by its owner, Sir John Stirling Maxwell, who brought an enthusiasm for architecture, as well as his skills as a horticul-

turist, to bear on the problems. The alterations had also to provide an appropriate setting for the important collection of Spanish paintings which Sir John had inherited. He employed Sir Rowand Anderson to supervise the additions but undoubtedly Sir John put forward his own suggestions. Although Anderson was recognised as the head of the architectural profession in Scotland, his mastery of period styles must have been an additional recommendation for Sir John who was anxious that the mid-Georgian character of the original villa on the outskirts of Glasgow should be preserved and respected in the additions.

Although the exterior of the house was restrained, the interiors like the Business Room possessed lively stucco decorations of the kind usually associated with

70b

William Adam to whom Sir John attributed the house. So skilfully could Anderson and his staff operate within historical idioms that it is quite difficult now to determine how much the original eighteenth-century interiors were helped along, but the Library, in one of the new flanking wings displays their ability to capture an eighteenth-century mood. The Venetian windows, like the Ionic order under its pulvinated frieze, were copied from the original house and the bays have been linked by idiosyncratic Scottish 'basket' arches. At Pollok not only are the light fittings designed to match but there seems to have been a serious attempt to follow the style through into the furnishings. To modern eyes the lack of textiles adds to the conviction but this seems to have been a personal idiosyncrasy of the owners because Sir John is said to have disliked carpets and his wife had tired of the perpetual washing of curtains that the grimy atmosphere of Glasgow necessitated.

The actual arrangement of the furniture, however, must be the photographer's temporary caprice since the pieces in the foreground of the library rendered traverse through the arch impossible. Rather in the spirit of Billings, *Country Life* eschewed dramatic lighting effects in favour of evenly lit, easily read spaces.

For clients who had not formed their own antique collection to demonstrate their good taste, or who did not trust their powers of Picturesque arrangement, Lorimer's team could supply the effect almost off-the-peg. Although this drawing is among Lorimer's papers in the National Monuments Record of Scotland, it actually came from Whytock and Reid, then as now the capital's premier firm of cabinet makers and upholsterers. Balmanno Castle, a sixteenth-century tower house, was renovated by Lorimer for W. S. Miller, a Glasgow shipping magnate, in 1916. The revived use of such detailed room plans seems to have been a French innovation, and Whytock and Reid had Parisian contacts. Before the Lorimer look came to dominate their output, they had made a speciality of revived French styles which had been made fashionable by the American novelist, Edith Wharton, whose book on decoration had made her the cynosure of international good taste.

The style of this Drawing Room, however, is home grown and reflects habits instilled by Rowand Anderson at his revolutionary Edinburgh School of Applied Art, which opened in 1892. His ideal was to establish an idiom of design based on the example of the past, and measured drawings of historic exemplars were central to the curriculum – an activity which Anderson believed was analogous to the study of anatomy in medical training. Pencil and delicate watercolour wash was the chosen medium (doubtless in deliberate opposition to the flashy Indian ink washes of the French Beaux Arts School) and soon became the norm as Anderson's young men were snapped up by Edinburgh's established firms. At Balmanno the Drawing Room was panelled but its Georgian style synthesised Carolean elements. Individually the furnishings are similarly eclectic but mustered together they supplied the same effect of quiet good taste with sufficient variety to dispel any sense of a 'twenty-guinea suite'. Although every item derives from antique prototypes, it is a tribute to Anderson's success that the pieces have a fluidity of line which, in combination with the firm's superb craftsmanship and fastidious choice of timbers, eclipsed the originals. The gossip chair is a further example of Lorimer's whimsical side. Even he had to make sacrifices in wartime because Whytock and Reid's proposal is unusually drawn on humble brown wrapping paper.

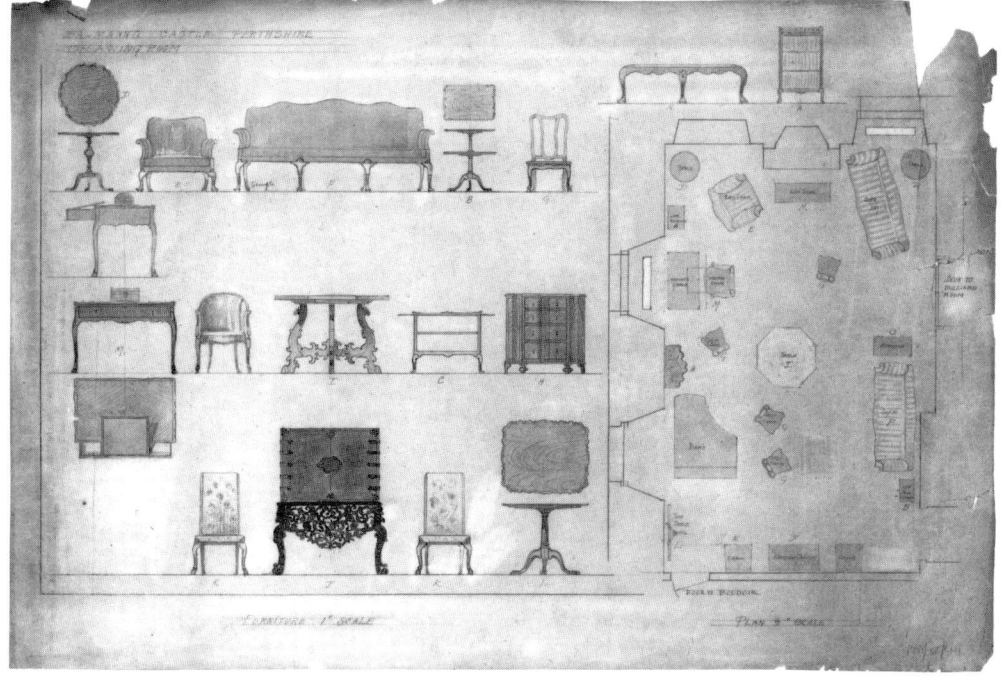

72: THE MATRON'S PRIVATE ROOM
AT THE PRINCESS LOUISE SCOTTISH HOSPITAL FOR LIMBLESS SAILORS
AND SOLDIERS AT ERSKINE HOUSE
1917

The Hospital was one of the largest charitable enterprises of the First World War and its opening was marked by a memorial volume illustrated with photographs by Annan which document an early reuse of a redundant country house, no longer required for family occupation. Erskine House had been designed by Sir Robert Smirke and was one of several houses offered to the Committee who were gratified that 'the Mansion House of much architectural beauty, has been preserved for one of the noblest purposes'. Great care was taken to preserve its historic character and 'the gas fittings of artistic and substantial design' were adapted for electricity. The Matron, Miss A. C. Douglas, is shown in her 'Private Room' whose efficiency with its capacious desk with two telephone lines and distempered walls has been tempered through the carpet, floral decorations and applied paper border below the frieze. The furniture follows a sensible traditional pattern with the exception of the high backed chairs in a restrained Glasgow style.

Scottish Country Life was a not particularly flattering imitation of its Southern namesake which had the misfortune to be founded on the eve of the First World War and its editor, George Eyre-Todd seems to have had difficulty in rising above the horizons of his advertisers. This absurd photograph was published in an article promoting the charms of the vicinity but is flagrantly an advertisement. Although many hotels had been converted from country houses and therefore came with a veneer of aristocratic furniture, this view is a reminder, when compared with the smart modernity of the Station Hotel at Perth, that the Duke of Gordon Hotel's 'famous collection of antiques and art furniture' had been recently assembled with an eye to impressing the now newly motorised passing tourist trade.

Although the enthusiasm for tower houses has shown no sign of abating throughout the twentieth century, there has been a growing impatience with the revived Baronial style's compromise between the Picturesque character of the ancient work and modern comforts. The rubble look is a consequence of this increasingly archaeological approach. Lennoxlove [74a,c] took its present form during a restoration by Lorimer in 1912–14 and it is revealing that Christopher Hussey records that Percy Macquoid, the doyen of English period furniture studies, acted as the advisor. In Hussey's understatement:

The Banqueting Hall as he left it is a notable example of a fifteenth-century interior untouched by intervening ages.

To late twentieth-century eyes the result has the drastic

74a

effect of an acid bath which has also, apparently, stripped the fur from the antlers. The rubble look has enjoyed very considerable popularity. It is frequently encountered in ancient houses like Glamis [74b] and usually carries with it the implication that an expensive Victorian Baronial phase has been expunged. A spectacular example can be found at Ford Castle in Northumberland which Bryce and Bonnar Baronialised for Louisa, Marchioness of Waterford. Leading a tour of the present interiors the late Colin McWilliam opened with the remarks 'You can see that the castle has received the attentions of the well known Scottish architects McStrippit and Pointit'.

7

74c

· 162 ·

An unfortunate consequence of early twentieth-century Scotland's ever increasing literacy in historical styles was a growing intolerance of buildings which reflect different periods of construction. As a result large sums of money have been self-righteously spent in ridding old buildings of their 'later alterations' with Victorian interiors taking first place on the casualty lists. Because Scotland's major contribution to interior decoration was made during the early Victorian period, the result has often been disastrous, as the Throne Room at Holyrood here demonstrates. The Palace found its champion in Queen Mary who was attracted by its fine Carolean plasterwork and antique furnishings, whose survival had been the result of Victorian parsimony. It was perhaps inevitable that the days of Matheson's Throne Room [31g] whose ceiling was described by the Queen as 'dreadful' should be numbered. However, not even the

Queen's enthusiasm could move the Treasury, who have no place on their balance sheet for taste, in spite of it being argued that the very 'dignity of Scotland' was at stake. Queen Mary had therefore to content herself with a Neo-Georgian redecoration. Hay's graining was overpainted in white; the walls were covered in 'period' damask and a suite of handsome gilt seat furniture was introduced. Agreement was secured, however, to devote the accumulated public admission charges to future renovation.

In 1929 a full Neo-Stuart refit was carried out under the direction of J. Wilson Paterson, of His Majesty's Office of Works in Scotland. A new ceiling was installed to reflect the character of the Charles II originals and sober oak panelling by Scott Morton and Co. incorporating paintings was applied to the walls The room was completed by a pair of new thrones. The result has never

75a

been considered a whole-hearted success. The room has merely been restyled without active consideration of the correct position for the different elements. As a result the room has absurdly continued to enshrine the purely temporary arrangements that prevailed for the State Visit of George IV in 1822. Because the King was not residing in the Palace, Charles II's room sequence was put into reverse so that the King could have exclusive use of the Great Stair. If Queen Mary's room relates stylistically to the adjacent rooms, it is a functional disaster and Holyrood must have the only Throne room in Europe where the sovereign sits with her back to the public route through the royal apartment.

Below: 75b

76: GEORGE DOBIE AND SON REDECORATE 94 GEORGE STREET, EDINBURGH 1925–39

George Dobie and Son's premises at 94 George Street reflect the vitality of this long established firm of Edinburgh decorators founded in 1849 and the photographs show it trying to shake off its Victorian ethos in favour of twentieth-century simplicity. The firm has always prided itself on the elegance of its premises and their shopfront at No. 94 remains the handsomest in George Street. It was installed in about 1930 to the designs of John B. P. Dobie who seems to have had some training with Lorimer. During the 1930s they pioneered the use of textured paints and new techniques.

76a

76b

76c

Montgomerie House was an exceptionally beautiful Neo-Classical country house designed in 1804 by John Paterson, who had acted as Robert Adam's Clerk of Works for some of his last Scottish commissions. This remarkably complete survey records its careful renovation during the 1930s which was doubtless motivated by a desire to remove all vestiges of the sumptuous Victorian decorative scheme recorded in photographs of 1895

[77a]. Some of the bedroom furniture must have been original to the house which was now equipped with every modern convenience. The record is the more poignant, because after a spell as an hotel, Montgomerie House was demolished in 1969 following damage by fire. Few of Scotland's lost country houses have been so well recorded.

77a

The National Monuments Record of Scotland was founded in May 1941, as the Scottish National Buildings Record. Its aim was to complete an emergency survey of our historic architecture in case of its destruction by enemy action, Although a high premium was placed on the collection of measured surveys, because of the shortage of draughtsmen resort had to be taken to the shortcut offered by existing topographical views, architectural drawings and measured surveys which is the origin of much of the material reproduced in this book. Happily Scotland's architecture came through the war relatively unscathed, but post-war reconstruction posed a more serious threat and thus the Record was permitted to continue its recording work.

In 1951 it was fortunate to attract as its Director a young English architect, the late Colin McWilliam, who brought to its work a fresh eye and a new enthusiastic professionalism. In view of the rate of destruction and the inadequacy of the Record's complement of staff, photography was the obvious medium. Although the traditional approach would have been to home in on the major architectural features of an interior such as its chimney-pieces and cornices Colin McWilliam's surveys show a real feeling for interiors and he made no attempt to edit his line of vision or to clear away the furnishings in the spirit of MacGibbon and Ross. The result is an idiosyncratic and unique collection which shows that through careful traditions of housekeeping, the nineteenth century still held Scotland in a firm grip as can be seen in these photographs of Skene House [78a], Corehouse [78b], Fettercairn House [78c] and Callendar House [78d]. Very few of these rooms were to survive the craze for modernisation that dominated the 1960s.

78a

b

78c

78d

79: A SCOTTISH HOME
1980s

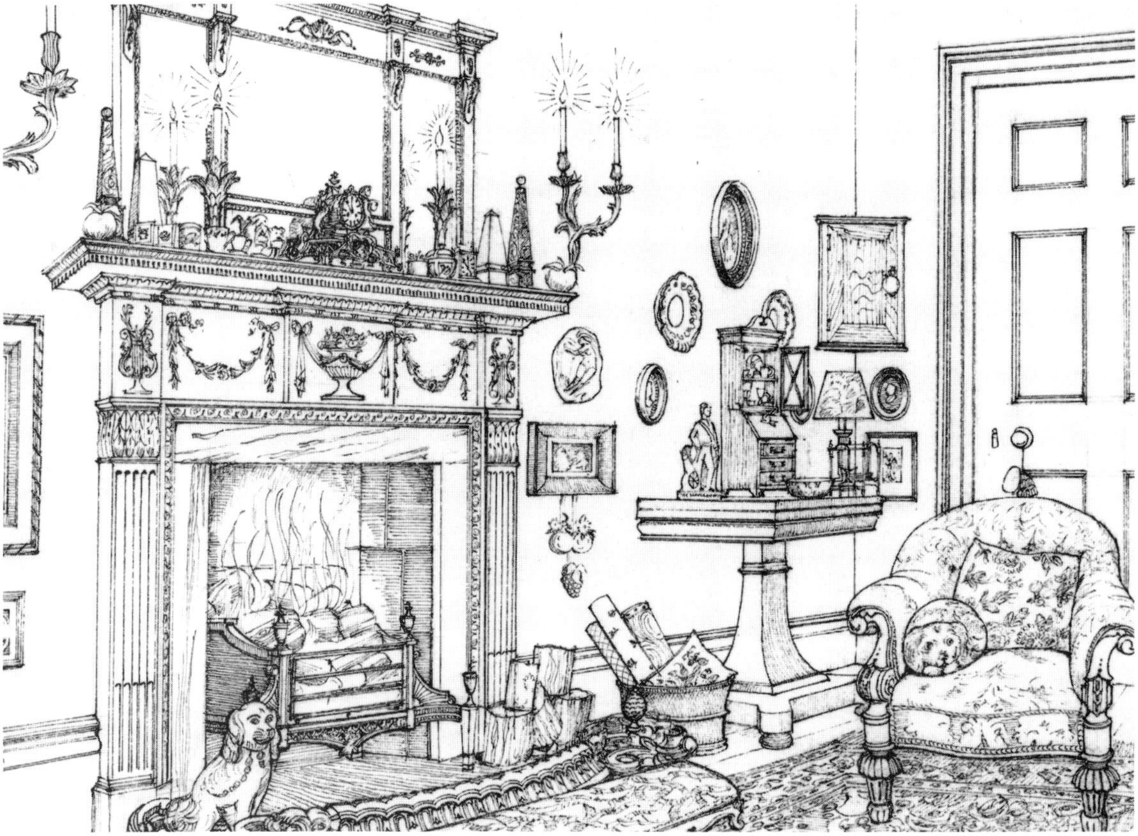

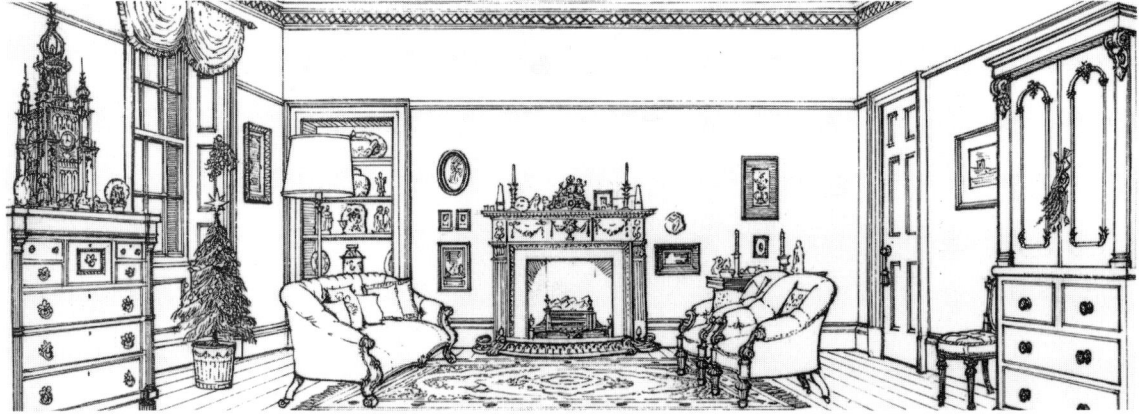

79a

79b

This book is as much about the history of the recording of Scottish interiors as the history of decoration in Scotland. If photography dominated the field almost from the time of its invention, these beautiful drawings form a fitting conclusion to this book because they show that, in the hands of a skilled artist, a drawing can still hold its own against the limitations of the camera. As the internal evidence reveals, these records were made as a series of Christmas cards and some have ingeniously placed folds. Although they show many Scottish elements, they are also a reminder of how the Scots have always selected what they required from Southern fashions as well as drawing on our native traditions.

79d

SELECT BIBLIOGRAPHY

Note: A more comprehensive listing of references to many of these buildings and artists is available through the catalogues of the National Monuments Record of Scotland.

1: George W T Omond, *Arniston Memoirs, 1571–1838*, 1887.

James Simpson, *Vitruvius Scoticus*, (reprint) 1980.

Mary Cosh, 'The Adam Family and Arniston', *Architectural History*, Volume 27, 1984 pp 214–225.

2: Arthur Oswald, 'Blair Castle, Perthshire', *Country Life* November 4 1949 pp 1362–1366; November 11 pp 1434–1438; November 18 pp 1506–1510.

4: T. Crouther Gordon, *David Allan, The Scottish Hogarth*, 1951.

6: Royal Commission on the Ancient and Historical Monuments Scotland, Argyll 5 *Islay, Jura, Colonsay and Oransay*, 1984.

7: Samuel Smiles (editor), *James Nasmyth Engineer an Autobiography*, 1897.

8: *Edinburgh in Olden Time*, 1880.

David Irwin, 'The Hermitage at Dunkeld "A Picturesque Experience"', *The Connoisseur*, November 1974.

9: William Park, 'Extracts from the Journal of Jessy Allan Wife of John Harden, 1801–1811', *The Book of the Old Edinburgh Club* Vol. XXX, 1959.

10: Lindsay Errington, *Alexander Carse*, (National Galleries of Scotland), 1987.

13: Francis Grant, Catalogue of the Pictures, *Ancient and Modern in Kinfauns Castle*, 1833 (printed by D Morison Perth).

Robert Speake, *Kinfauns Castle*, 1982.

John Cornforth, 'Scone Palace, Perthshire', *Country Life*, August 11 1988 pp 92–96 and August 18 pp 72–76.

16: Lindsay Errington, *Tribute to Wilkie*, (National Galleries of Scotland), 1985.

W F Watson, *Edinburgh Its Houses and Its Noted Inhabitants* (Architectural Institute of Scotland), 1865.

17: J G Lockhart, *Memoirs of the Life of Sir Walter Scott Bart.*, 1842.

D R Hay, *The Laws of Harmonious Colouring adapted to Interior Decorations*, sixth edition, 1847.

Clive Wainwright, 'Abbotsford House, Roxburgh-shire', *Country Life*, June 8 1989 pp 262–167.

18: The Marquess and Marchioness of Aberdeen, *We Twa, Reminiscences of Lord and Lady Aberdeen*, 1925.

Christopher Hussey, 'Haddo House, Aberdeenshire', *Country Life* , August 18 1966 pp 378–381 and August 25 pp 448–452.

19: Elizabeth, Duchess of Northumberland (editor James Greig), *The Diaries of a Duchess, Extracts From the Diary of the First Duchess of Northumberland, 1716–1776*, 1926.

Anon., *Historical Description of the Monastery or Chapel Royal of Holyroodhouse with a Short Account of the Palace and Environs*, 1818.

Margaret Swain, *Tapestries and Textiles at the Palace of Holyroodhouse*, (HMSO), 1988.

20: Ian Gow, *The Northern Athenian House* (unpublished lecture, typescript in NMRS).

21: John Milne, *Description of Sir John Robison's House*, 1840.

22: Alistair Rowan, 'Taymouth Castle, Perthshire', *Country Life*, October 8 1964 pp 912–916 and October 15 pp 978–981.

Dorothy Bosomworth, 'A Royal Tour', *Traditional Interior Decoration* October–November 1987 pp 72–78.

23: *Edinburgh in Olden Time*, 1880.

James Colston, *Trinity College and Trinity Hospital, An Historical Sketch, 1896.*

Nicholas N M'Q Holmes, *Trinity College Church, Hospital, Apse, History and Architecture* (City of Edinburgh Museums and Art Galleries), 1988.

24: R W Billings, 'Certain Features of the Ancient Architecture of Scotland', *Proceedings of the Architectural Institute of Scotland*, 10 March 1853.

25: Margaret Noel-Paton, *Tales of a Grand-daughter*, 1970.

Adolph Cavallo, *Joseph Neil Paton: Designer of Damasks, The Connoisseur*, Vol CLIII, 1963.

26: Ronald W Clark, *Balmoral Queen Victoria's Highland Home*, 1981.

Delia Millar, *Queen Victoria's Life in the Scottish Highlands*, 1985.

29: Robert Strathearn Lindsay, *A History of the Mason's Lodge of Holyrood House (St Luke's No 44)*, 1935.

31: Ian Gow, 'Elegance on a Shoe-string, Queen Victoria at Holyrood', *Country Life*, July 30 1987 pp 126–129 and August 6 pp 76–79.

34: J Marley Hay, *The Scenery of the Dee*, (illustrated by Andrew Gibb), 1884.

35: Elspeth Gallie, 'Glasgow's Most Elegant House', *Scottish Field*, August 1959 pp. 22–23.

36: Sheila Forman, 'The Place of Auchinleck', *Scotland's Magazine* , November 1952.

Robertson Sutherland, *Loanhead*, 1974.

Ian Gow, 'Mavisbank, Midlothian', *Country Life*, August 20 1987 pp 70–73.

38: Ronald McFadzean, *The Life and Work of Alexander Thomson*, 1979.

H W Fincham, 'Greek Thomson's Double Villa', *Architect's Journal* 19 February 1986 pp 36–50.

39: *Scottish Country Life*, Volume VII No 12 December 1920, pp 523–528.

42: A L Simpson, *In Memoriam Thomas Bonnar*, 1876.

Thomas Bonnar, *Notes on the Present Art Revival*, 1879.

43: *The Hamilton Palace Collection* Sale Catalogue, in their rooms, Christie's, London June 17-June 19, 1882.

The Hamilton Palace Collection Illustrated Priced Catalogue, 1882.

Hamilton Palace Remaining Contents, on the premises Christie's Wednesday November 12 1919.

G A Walker, *Hamilton Palace: A Photographic Record*, 1976.

A A Tait, 'The Duke of Hamilton's Palace', *The Burlington Magazine*, Volume CXXV July 1983 pp 394–402.

44: John Marshall, *Amateur House Decoration*, (Edinburgh Architectural Association), 1883.

45: Sheila Forman, 'Cullen', *Scotland's Magazine*, June 1954, pp 30–33.

Valerie Fiddes and Alistair Rowan, *David Bryce 1803–1876*, 1976.

46: David Walker, 'The Architecture of MacGibbon and Ross: The Background to the Books', *Studies in Scottish Antiquity* (editor David Breeze), 1984 pp 391–449.

48: *Catalogue to the Collections*, (Burns Cottage-Museum), 1922.

49: TBM, *Slum Life in Edinburgh or Scenes in its Darkest Places*, 1891.

50: John A Fairley, *Lauriston Castle*, 1925.

53: Cosmo Monkhouse, 'A Northern Home', (reprinted from the *Art Journal*), 1897.

Elspeth Hardie, 'William Scott Morton', *The Antique Collector*, March 1988, pp 70–79.

54: Harriet Richardson, *Kellie Castle*, St Andrew's University M.Litt Dissertation (unpublished), 1986.

Peter Savage, *Lorimer and the Edinburgh Craft Designers*, 1980.

56: A H Millar, 'Kinnaird', *The Castles and Mansions of Scotland, Perthshire and Forfarshire*, 1890.

59: *Montrave House*, Sale Catalogue, on the premises, Thomas Love and Sons, Perth, June 24th–26th 1929.

61: Cassel and Co., *Historic Houses of the United Kingdom*, 1891, pp 170–183.

A Catalogue of the Valuable Contents of Culloden House, Sale catalogue, Wednesday 21st July, 1897 A. Fraser and Co., Inverness.

62: Sam McKinstry, *Rowand Anderson: 'The Premier Architect of Scotland'*, Edinburgh University Press, 1991.

65: Christopher Hussey, *The Work of Sir Robert Lorimer*, 1931.

'Earlshall, Fife' *Country Life*, Volume XVIII July 1 1905, pp 942–952.

66: Nicholas Cooper, *The Opulent Eye*, 1976.

65: Andrew Paterson, *Some Reminiscences of an Uneventful Life, A Fragment*, with a continuation of the Story of his Life and an Appreciation of his Personality by his Youngest Son Alexander Nisbet Paterson, 1937–38. (unpublished manuscript, photocopy in NMRS.)

67: Peter Savage. Lorimer and the Edinburgh Craft Designers, 1980.

68: Patrick J Ford, '*Interior Paintings*' by Patrick W. Adam, RSA, 1920.

70: Lawrence Weaver, 'Pollok House, Renfrewshire', *Country Life*, Volume XXXIII 1913 p 126.

Juliet Kinchin, *Pollok House*, 1983.

74: Clive Aslet, 'Lennoxlove, East Lothian', *Country Life*, Volume CLXXVIII 1985 pp 366–70, 446–9.

76: W. M. Parker, *Dobie and Son. Ltd, 1849–1949*, 1949.

77: A H Millar, *Castles and Mansions of Ayrshire*, 1884.

78: RCAHMS, NMRS Jubilee, *A Guide to the Collections*, 1991.

PHOTOGRAPHIC CREDITS

The following illustrations have been reproduced by gracious permission of Her Majesty the Queen: 26a–d and 31a–g.

The remaining illustrations are reproduced courtesy of:

His Grace the Duke of Atholl, 2

The British Architectural Library, 21a–b

His Grace the Duke of Buccleuch and Queensberry, fig 4

The Courtauld Institute of Art, 63

Country Life, 70

Edinburgh City Museums (Lauriston Castle Collection), 50

The Company of Merchants of the City of Edinburgh, 23

Edinburgh Public Libraries, 49b

The University of Edinburgh, Department of Fine Art, 57

Edinburgh University Library, Special Collections Department, 67

Hamilton District Libraries, 43

The Earl of Mansfield, 13b

The Mitchell Library, Glasgow, 3

The National Gallery of Scotland, 4 (including [4c] known as 'The Penny Wedding'), 7, 16, 17

The National Library of Scotland, fig 2, 9, 14, 46a–b

The National Trust for Scotland, 18, 24f

The Sandeman Library, Perth, 13c–e

Private Collections, figs 5 and 6, 1, 5, 10, 20, 25, 27, 28, 30, 35, 36a–c, 39, 42b–c, 49c, 55b, 56, 61a, 61b, 76, 77, 79

The Royal Commission on the Ancient and Historical Monuments of Scotland (The National Monuments Record of Scotland), p4, p7, fig 3, 6, 8, 11, 12, 13a, 15, 19, 21c–d, 22, 24a–g, 26e–g, 31g, 32, 37, 38, 40, 41, 42, 44, 46c, 47, 48, 49a, 51, 52, 53, 54, 55a, 58, 59, 60, 61c, 62d, 65, 66, 68, 69, 71, 72, 73, 74, 75, 78

The Royal Incorporation of Architects in Scotland, 62, 64

The Scottish National Portrait Gallery, 34

The Scottish Record Office, 29

Spink and Son Ltd, London, 33